Syr

Marissa Ohara and Charles Lyons are freelance musicians, working in the casino orchestras in Las Vegas in the 1970s. They are among a handful of classically trained string players in the bands that backed the popular singers of the day: Frank Sinatra, Dean Martin, Sammy Davis Jr., Bob Goulet, Shirley MacLaine, etc. The bands were basically Big Band, and the added strings produced rich symphonic sounds to enhance these idols' spectacular shows.

Marissa and Charlie form a close friendship that eventually leads to marriage. The reader is taken behind the scenes of the workplace—backstage and the band rooms—to see the interaction between the players and the stars who were idols in the then-flourishing music business.

In 1970 Las Vegas was just a budding desert town. It had a small branch of the University of Nevada where Charlie enrolled as candidate for a doctorate in Nevada history. He supported himself while in college by continuing to play in the Strip orchestras. Marissa lived with him and worked full time in the casino bands for the big stars who appeared nonstop for two decades.

Marissa Ohara is not Irish, as her last name might suggest. Rather she is full-blooded Japanese, but thoroughly American by birth and upbringing. Marissa's father, George Shigeo Ohara, a second-generation American, was in his senior year at the University of California at Berkeley when Pearl Harbor was attacked.

Through Charlie's knowledge of history Marissa becomes aware of her parent's wartime subjugation. She also learns about the life of the Japanese immigrant in California in the early 1900s: how people of her parents' and grandparents' generations came to America, and how they were denied social and economic advancement available to their white fellow citizens.

This book also tells of the 120,000 innocent Japanese-American men, women, and children uprooted from their homes during the war, with details about the evacuation and the three years they were forced to live in barbed wire camps. These stories are drawn from the writer's own experience as one of those internees.

ALLEGRO
A FICTIONALIZED MEMOIR

Helene Honda

For Marlene and Jerry Drbe

Fond memories

Helene Honda

Park Place Publications
Pacific Grove, California

2014

ALLEGRO: A FICTIONALIZED MEMOIR

Helene Honda
stories.eiko@yahoo.com

Cover photo of Eiko Ceremony by S. Yoshizato

ISBN 978-1-935530-73-2

Printed in U.S.A.
Available from Amazon.com

First U.S. Edition: December 2012

Edited by Cindie Farley
Text design by Patricia Hamilton
Cover design by Cheryl Puckett
Cover images from Vince DiBiase
and Photos.com: flag–onur ersin, fan–Roksana Bashyrova, barbed wire–Chris Sadowski

Published by
Park Place Publications
Pacific Grove, California
www.parkplacepublications.com

Prologue

As the show neared its end every musician in the 45-piece orchestra blasted out the last notes of the finale: the winds and brasses blowing hard with their last breath, fiddle-players digging their bows into their instruments, and—at the top row of the bandstand—the drummer furiously pounding his tymps, his assistant having a field day dazzling the audience with each cymbal clash. After a moment of stunned silence the crowd rose to its feet, cheered and whistled louder than the last echo from the orchestra.

Burt Bacharach and Anthony Newley came out for one curtain call after another, waved, bowed, and threw kisses to the audience as the applause reached an even higher pitch.

The elated expressions on faces were rare indeed, as strangers applauded, cheered, smiled, and felt as one. They could not stop, but knowing that all good things must come to an end they watched the elegant red velvet curtains drop down onto the boards, while behind the curtains the relieved musicians stood up, anxious to get off the bandstand.

Burt and Tony turned to the band and waved. "Thanks guys, and ladies, too!"

"Our pleasure … good show," the band shouted back, the guys giving thumbs up.

Burt and Anthony exited the silenced stage that only a few moments before was filled with their magic. The musicians in formal black loosened their bow ties, relaxed their serious demeanor and muttered "Fooled 'em again!" and "Finally get to play some good music!" while the women among them swooned, "Oh-h, isn't Tony cute? I bet he's a devil. Yum!"

These two men were royalty among the entertainers who performed in the showrooms of Las Vegas in the 1970s.

◆

PART 1 SCHERZO

Marissa and Charlie in Las Vegas

Chapter 1

Another successful opening night! Well-dressed women and men streamed out of the Las Vegas showroom into the huge casino, chatting and smiling with satisfaction over the first-rate dinner and entertainment they had just enjoyed. Their voices melted into the noise of the casino, already packed with gamblers, drinkers, and employees.

Onstage, behind the curtain, musicians stepped out of their roles as performers and once again became plain folk. Much relieved, they started to leave one by one, the men loosening their black ties, and the women chattering about the handsome men in the audience. Stagehands dimmed the lights after the last musician left, wiping away any hint of glamour that had illuminated the stage moments ago.

Clutching her violin, Marissa Ohara rushed to the band room from where other musicians were already hurrying out for the two-hour break. Carefully putting her violin away she wondered, *Should I stay here and watch the ten o'clock news, or go to the coffee shop? Egads, the guys are already pulling beer out of the fridge so it's going to get noisy in here, but the restaurant would be too crowded. Oh, how I'd love a cup of coffee, though. Best thing to do is to go outside and see if Charlie might be strolling on the Strip too. He takes walks after playing at Caesar's Palace. Yeah, that sounds like the best thing to do.*

Marissa and Charlie Lyons frequently bumped into one another on the street after working at their respective hotels. She knew that when musicians worked together to reach exacting ensemble-playing and experiencing a veritable high, they needed time and space to float back to reality.

Out in the casino now Marissa was caught up in the crowd shuffling toward the coffee shop, when she stopped herself. *Mmm. Some woman has on a wonderful perfume, smells like Shalimar. Mmm, nice. . . Oops, don't want to go here to the coffee shop.* It seemed to be the place for musicians and music contractors to talk shop, and she didn't want to get caught up in that. *"I'd better follow the crowd to the lobby and out into the street. Fresh air and a change of scenery are what I need.*

Hungrily inhaling the fresh air, Marissa saw multi-colored lights filling the night sky as they flashed at the Dunes across the street. The marquee was enticing people to see the show with dancers direct from Paris, and the street was almost as bright as daytime with nearby buildings also highly lit. Row upon row of flashing colored lights tricked the senses into accepting this phony daylight exposing pedestrians on the prowl. They eyeballed each other, men hungrily staring at provocative female bodies walking around in tight dresses, and women stealing glances at certain men, fantasizing what it would be like to be in their arms. Little old ladies with plastic cups holding their winnings from one casino's slot machines to the next enjoyed their girl's night out—having had free drinks in each hotel added to their merriment. Traffic was gridlocked along the entire five-mile Strip, especially at Flamingo and Las Vegas Boulevard, where Marissa was waiting with the pedestrians to cross the street. The dinner shows in every major hotel had ended, letting a thousand people from each showroom loose to join the throng in the streets. Marissa melded into this mass movement, grateful for her anonymity there, the next best thing to being alone.

The Caesar's Palace entrance with its fountains was dwarfed by their gigantic marquee announcing Frank Sinatra. *Hmm, I wonder which fiddle players are in the band. Sinatra uses a big string section. If I see Charlie he'll bring me up-to-date.*

Approaching the Flamingo Hotel, she checked its marquee. *Marty Allen. Funny, friendly guy. Uses a small 15-piece band. Not much music needed with a stand-up comic.*

"Hey, Marissa!" called a young man in a black suit striding briskly toward her, his smile causing her heart to skip a beat.

"Oh, hi, Charlie," she smiled, trying to sound blasé. Charlie Lyons was a violist in the Caesar's Palace show band, and like her he was out for a breather.

"I was wondering if you'd be out for a walk too," he said, happy to see her. They had to raise their voices to be heard over the street noise.

"Boy, am I glad that first Sinatra show is over."

"We did a great one with Bacharach and Newley," Marissa responded. "Playing for two big stars is demanding, but lots of good music."

"C'mon, Marissa, let's get to a quiet place." Smiling and taking her by the elbow, he pointed toward the back of the Flamingo Hotel, "Let's go there, outside to the pool area. It's quieter and darker so we can relax away from the neon and madness."

Hmm, this is new. We usually just stop, chat briefly, and then go on our separate ways. What's with him tonight?

The pair made their way quickly through the crowded smoke-filled casino with slot machines clanging away. They were an attractive pair, both in their mid-twenties, she Oriental and petite, he Caucasian, with chestnut brown hair, tall and almost handsome. They knew their black outfits gave them away as musicians on a break, and that the ever-alert security guards might spot them making their way toward the pool. All around, bells and whistles blasted out from slot machines hitting jackpots, with crowds of people straining to see how much was won. Scantily clad cocktail waitresses maneuvered around with loaded drink trays, men and women ogled each other, the men making motions to pinch the bottoms of the females sashaying about. All this a fleeting glimpse of people away from their boring, circumscribed lives in small-town U.S.A., doing things here that they would never dare think of doing back home.

"Whew, the Strip's swinging tonight," said Charlie. "I had to fight my way out of the Caesar's Palace casino. Sinatra brings in high rollers, you know."

"That's why I don't go home between shows," said Marissa. "Too many musicians have been injured driving back home between shows … so many drunks on the road!"

"Yeah, that's why I stay around too," said Charlie, looking around the noisy crowd.

Charlie and Marissa had worked together on other jobs, and enjoyed each other's cordial company. Neither knew much about the other, only that they had both come to Vegas after learning that salaries here were double what small symphony orchestras paid.

Behind the casino they entered a large, dimly lit garden with flowerbeds lining the walkways. After adjusting their eyes to the semi-darkness, they found a little table near the pool where several other couples were seated, holding hands and speaking softly.

Charlie and Marissa sighed with relief as they sank into their chairs while a lone swimmer did laps back and forth. Incredibly, just beyond the adjacent wall was the brightness and din of the Las Vegas Strip at the height of the evening. The sudden quiet in this darkened backyard atmosphere seemed a soothing balm to Marissa and Charlie, along with just gazing into the water of the pool.

"Opening night's a bitch," Charlie grumbled, closing his eyes and sighing again.

"Yes, nearly killed me the first few months I worked in this town," Marissa replied. *And always before my periods.*

"Been here a year, so I'm used to it now."

A cocktail waitress came by and chanted "Cock-tails... cocktails?"

"Oh, I'd love some coffee, black, please," said Marissa.

"The same for me, too."

More delicious silence. This was better than going home and getting too settled in, then having to drive back to play a second show from midnight to two a.m.

"Charlie, where did you study?"

"I got my Master's from SC in American History, but did a lot of playing there as a music minor. Good music department. You know how a violist is always in demand. Don't mean to put you down, but violin players are a dime a dozen. Anyway, I didn't want to go into teaching after graduation, so I feel lucky doing something I also love, scratching on the fiddle and getting paid for it. My daytime hours are free, so I can do my history research." He hesitated, wondering if he was talking too much about himself, this being the first time he'd talked to Marissa at length. "I want to do graduate studies somewhere—even here."

"You're making good use of your free time, Charlie," Marissa said with admiration in her voice. "I'm not sure I like this town, but with work calls coming in regularly I'll stay a while. During my free time I putter around in the garden patio behind my apartment. Of course, I always get in some serious practice too, and after that if I want to go anywhere, it's either the casinos, Lake Mead, or the Red Rock Mountains. I'm not a moviegoer. Not much choice."

"Trouble with Vegas is the scarcity of places to go when you're not working," said Charlie. "Back in LA, there was always something going on: good plays, lectures, hanging out in cafes, the Philharmonic concerts, and then those museums—absolutely fabulous . . .Where's home, Marissa?"

"In Monterey, south of San Francisco. My dad is teaching

and Mom works at a gift shop. Oh, how I loved going to San Francisco all the time and walking around North Beach and the bookstores and cafes. I even played impromptu concerts and met a lot of musicians at the Spaghetti Factory. I also did a few summers with the orchestra at the Carmel Bach Festival; but you know, with just a diploma from Juilliard and no degree, all I did was freelance. I could have taken on private students, but I'm like you. I don't care to teach. Ties me down too much."

"So you've played in all kinds of places, huh?"

"Yes, I did lots of tours which was exciting at first. The Metropolitan Opera sent a road company out around the country, even into Canada and Mexico. That went on for two years until the road manager absconded with the funds." She chuckled recalling the abrupt ending of a promising long-term musical engagement. "You ever do any tours Charlie?"

"Naw, I like to stay put in one place. I'm here because I got called when they ran short of string players for Perry Como, and they've kept me on."

"Funny, isn't it, how life springs weird surprises on us? I landed here when someone from the opera tour recommended me for a gig with Wayne Newton. He uses a big string section."

"Oh, him." Charlie rolled his eyes. "You gotta give him credit, though; he works hard and his shows go over big with folks who like cornball."

"Did you know, Charlie, there was a nun who came in every night to see him? Sat right up front and blushed whenever he talked to her. One shopkeeper told me that her out-of-town customers won't come to Las Vegas unless Wayne is appearing … No accounting for other people's tastes, eh?"

"He has that kind of following?" Charlie shook his head. "Oh, well, it takes all kinds."

The waitress brought their coffees. As they sipped slowly they got the kick they needed for the midnight show … and also enjoyed getting to know each other.

"Tell me, Marissa, are you Japanese? Your name looks Irish though. Ohara, isn't it?"

"Yes, how'd you guess? Most people say 'Chinese' when we first meet. My last name is pronounced *Ohh-Hara*. It's a real Japanese name."

"Interesting. My mom had Japanese friends who visited us now and then."

"Thank goodness, you're familiar with us Orientals." Encouraged with his understanding, Marissa said somberly, "It's so painful when the redneck clerks here talk to me slowly with raised voices and want to see my ID."

"Yeah, I think I know what you mean. L.A. is a cosmopolitan city, and being a port city, we see lots of foreigners. I had Japanese classmates all through school, we grew up alongside each other. I even had a Japanese teacher in third grade, Miss Sato. A couple of times I went with Mom to her Japanese friend's home. The house had a plain exterior with no hint that it would be filled with exotic furniture. Teak, I guess, with silk pillows, and embroidered tablecloths and delicate silk scrolls on the walls. One time they were burning incense. It gave me a feeling of being in a strange, magical land."

Marissa and Charlie continued to chitchat, grateful that each understood the other's need to unwind with someone of like mind.

After a few stretches of silence or staring at the water, Charlie looked at his watch, stretched his arms, leaned forward and said, "I gotta go soon, but I have another question. It's about something in my field of interest." He hesitated before asking. "Were your folks ever in those camps during the war? I did a term project on it and wanted to become a civil rights lawyer after researching and writing that report."

Marissa paused before saying, "Yes, my folks and grandparents were all in those American concentration camps."

Charlie perked up. "Gee, I wish I'd known them when I was doing that paper."

Marissa said, "Charlie, my dad kept a pretty good record of his imprisonment. No one talks about it, but I was planning to ask him and Mom some day about those four or five terrible years. Next time I go home, I can bring it up. I myself don't know too much about what went on, though."

"Well, find out if they are in the mood to talk about it. Wartime is awful, so please don't push it, okay? … I had to do a lot of digging for information because people didn't talk about it, and everyone was too busy rebuilding their lives after the war. That's a period of American history that's always bothered me and I want to make a more detailed study of it."

Charlie continued, " I'm still undecided about what period of American History I want to specialize in. It's been a toss-up between American Indian history, or an in-depth study of Nevada."

"Nevada?" asked Marissa with surprise.

"Oh, yeah." He said enthusiastically. "This is a young state and there are still people living who are only a generation or two away from its founding. I find that exciting, and know that talking with these pioneers' descendants will make history come alive. You know, it won't be just a list of names and places."

"Oh, for me history has always been memorizing dates and places and names of dead people." *He's going to think I'm really stupid.*

"I had a good teacher in high school who got me

interested when we were doing American Indian studies. That's when I found out there were Indian ancestors in my dad's family a few generations back."

Charlie looked at his watch and stood up. "I don't know about you, but I want to get back to work a little early. You know how it is on opening night, the way they make program changes if they weren't happy with something in the first show." As they started walking to the street Charlie said, "Listen, Marissa, once our shows start running on automatic, let's meet at the Dunes Coffee shop for late supper some night."

"All right, Charlie, that sounds great," she replied as they reluctantly left the tranquility of their poolside retreat.

Crossing the noisy street on the way to their respective hotels, each wondered why the other was still apparently unattached.

Chapter 2

Overton

After his gig at Caesar's there were no work calls for a couple of weeks, and Charlie planned a drive along the Virgin River, just north from Las Vegas. There, in the little townships, he could check out the old Mormon settlements and talk to any descendants of the original settlers to gather firsthand information for his thesis. This would keep his mind focused on a goal. Playing music was fine, but history was of deeper interest for his life's work. The music would always be there within him, and he could always work in the bands to support himself while he continued his studies at the university.

With such a plan forming in his mind, he wanted to bounce these ideas around with someone. His family and college friends were miles away in Los Angeles. The only person at work who might understand him would be Marissa—or so he wished. But would she be interested? He had nothing to lose if he casually mentioned his hopes to her. He dialed her number.

"Hey, Marissa, how are you? It's a nice day. How about a ride to Overton? It's a couple of hours away from here."

Marissa was surprised and pleased to hear from him. "Oh hi, Charlie. I've never heard of Overton. Sure, I'd love to go, in fact, I *need* to get away after playing that loud music for the Jackson Five, and it's too nice a day to be cooped up inside. Gee, that's a good idea."

"Cool. I'll pick you up shortly, and we'll drive by some of the old Mormon settlements and stop at the Lost City museum. Even in the desert, if we look hard enough, there are interesting places, I'll show you."

"That's so good of you, Charlie. I'll be ready by the time you get here."

The idea of being with Marissa gave Charlie a pleasant anticipation of a nice day off. When she came out of her apartment, Charlie thought, *How attractive she is when she smiles. How graceful and reserved*, he thought, as he opened the car door for her.

"I know this is selfish, Marissa," he said, as they were driving along the desert highway, loving her black pony-tailed hair flying in the wind. "Where we're going is of historical interest to me, but at the same time, you might see something different."

Marissa, enjoying the sunshine and the openness of the desert, said, "This is wonderful, Charlie. What a big relief to find that life goes on normally once outside that pleasure-seeking atmosphere of the Strip." Stretching her arms up, "Ah-h, now I'm beginning to feel sane, more normal with each mile we get away from there."

"You and me both," he said smiling, drawing in a deep breath. *Good. I made a point with her. I was pretty sure she didn't care for the party mood all over the Strip.* They rode in silence, lost in thought and glad to be escaping from people in pursuit of sensational pleasures.

Marissa felt fortunate that Charlie showed this much interest in her. She knew he could have taken out other girls he knew at work.

Soon little houses, more like shacks, came into view. Charlie slowed down until they came to a cluster of one-story buildings on both sides of the highway, with the American flag flying over one. "Here we are, the Lost City Museum."

"Oh, Charlie, what quaint buildings, and that one with a wooden ladder to get to the roof. It's so different. Oh my, I love the bright pink adobe walls on that one."

Surprisingly, there were several cars in the parking lot.

"See," said Charlie, "Even on a weekday, tourists come here." They entered a lobby with glass cases displaying old pottery and masks. A group of men were clustered around a case containing axes, stone knives, and arrows. "We'll come back to this section later," said Charlie, realizing that they would not be able to get close enough to the display cases to get a better view of the objects.

They entered another room filled with old Pueblo remains that had been found in the area. "Now, look here at these remains, Marissa," said Charlie masterfully, pointing to various objects displayed in the cases. "The Pueblos lived here until a lake dried up, and they moved elsewhere. See how different they crafted their vases and utensils? Different from the Paiutes who were here when the Mormons came in the 1850's" He seemed to be interested in the detailed differences that Marissa could not really see.

Standing by a showcase, Marissa was admiring the craftwork of the long-gone Pueblo tribe: vases, grinding stones, pieces of leather clothing, arrowheads, and crude utensils. She turned to Charlie to make a comment when she noticed with surprise that his demeanor had changed. He was no longer just the serious musician she always perceived him to be; now, he appeared to be a probing scientist. *Why, he's like a methodical chemist bending over the results of a new formula.*

"Do you mind if I talk to the curator, Marissa?" Charlie pointed to a door down the hallway. "I want to ask him a few questions about the Pueblo Indians who once lived in this region."

"Go ahead, Charlie, I'll keep looking at the other exhibits. My, but it's so interesting here."

Marissa had been jolted when she caught this glimpse of another Charlie. She was hardly able to concentrate on the unusual items on display as she walked from one case to another. *He is a very scholarly man, perhaps a little prodding; but strangely, he appeals to me.*

A half hour later Charlie emerged from the door of the curator's office, beaming and clutching several sheets of notes.

"Sorry to keep you waiting, Marissa, but I got more information than I expected. Let's go to that diner across the road, and I'll tell you some of the things he told me."

After being seated in the restaurant, Charlie said brightly, "Marissa, this has been a productive day for me already."

"It must have been like discovering treasures, when you got to talk to the curator," Marissa said encouragingly.

"Oh, yeah. Since moving to Las Vegas, I've been excited playing for big-name singers, one after another, but musically, it's not as satisfying as doing classical music, the meaty stuff, you know."

"Sure," agreed Marissa wholeheartedly. "We all feel that way, but we're caught up in commercial work, and wonder of wonders, as musicians, we're able to make a good living."

"How long will that last? Anyway, I told you I wanted to go for a doctorate in Nevada History, and that idea's been gnawing at me lately. It's going to take a few years to delve into the history of this area, all aspects of it, the original inhabitants, the archeological findings, the first white settlers, and the people who established Las Vegas. I can support myself playing music while I do the studies. Doesn't that sound good to you?"

Marissa thought it over. *He's come to a fork in the road.* She told him slowly and deliberately, "You seem to have a clear goal in mind … . I'd say 'go for it.' The time's right when your enthusiasm's this strong."

Gratefully, this was what Charlie had hoped to hear, words of encouragement in her softly-spoken manner. "I'm not going to waste any more time. I've already checked out the history department at UNLV and I want to start as soon as I can. Of course, after that, there are going to be deeper studies, but I hope to get grants."

"You've been thinking about this a lot, haven't you?"

"Un, huh. In spite of what Las Vegas appears to be, after scratching the surface, I'm finding that this area hasn't been thoroughly studied. Did I tell you that on my Dad's side there are some Indian ancestors back in Ohio? Mom's family is old California from over a century ago."

The waiter came to take their order. "What'll it be, folks?"

Marissa looked up at the menu board, "You have a vegetable special that sounds good."

"Yes, ma'am. They're grown locally by a Japanese settler from way back … that would be Mr. Tomiyasu. Ever hear of him? He used to own a big ranch in Las Vegas." The waiter hesitated before saying, "You look like you might be Japanese, ma'am."

"Yes, I'm from California. Uh, I never heard of Mr. Tomiyasu, though."

"Mr. Tomiyasu's been here for ages, grew the best vegetables for the town when they were building the Hoover Dam back in the 30s, and later during the war, for the Air Force base. This way, we didn't need to have fresh vegetables shipped from California." The waiter turned to Charlie, asking, "And what would you like, sir?"

Charlie ordered farm-style meat and vegetables.

"See, Marissa, these stories you stumble onto about the old-timers? It can be lots of fun."

"Gosh, this being a historian can be exciting, Charlie. I never knew it'd be like this."

Back at home that night Marissa called Charlie to thank him for the lovely day, assuring him how much she enjoyed the trip to Overton.

Charlie went to bed full of satisfaction with the day's events, and being able to be with a woman who made him feel at ease. *She makes me like myself when I'm with her.*

Before falling asleep Marissa thought about Charlie's well laid-out plans for his future. He needed a boost, which she felt she gave. His life would be a quiet one, with small, satisfying moments like today. Her gut instinct told her he was the kind of man suitable for her temperament. Being with him might turn out to be a good life for both of them.

What in the world was she thinking, "both of them?" *Get a hold of yourself. Right now you're just his sounding board. Remember that, girl.*

The following day Marissa called Charlie again to thank him for the most enjoyable day off. He didn't seem to mind getting another phone call from her. "Charlie, I feel so refreshed after getting away from here. You know, I got to thinking about your studies. Some day, I'd like to show you my father's notes of his war experiences. It isn't directly connected with your major study, but somewhere along the line, it may serve some purpose."

"Gee, Marissa, that's generous of you to offer me something that special." His heart was jumping. "Of course, I would love to read his notes. This way, I can delve into the evacuation of the Japanese from California during the war … Yeah, thanks, Hon, but don't you think your dad would mind your asking him about such a traumatic time in his life?"

After some consideration Marissa wrote to her father asking about his diary of wartime experiences. Her father was reluctant at first to revive unpleasant memories of those years, but at the same time was heartened that Marissa was showing interest about her own family background, especially that chapter in American history—a shameful one—he recalled bitterly. Then, quickly, he felt grateful that Marissa was born after that, and was spared the hardships he and his parents endured. Even if he would have to relive memories of that chaotic period, perhaps after all these years, he may be able to resolve in his own mind the many things that he had buried. To dredge them up and look at them more objectively with the present day's perspective on those events of long ago would be a good tonic for the psyche. He went up to the attic.

Chapter 3

The following Monday, instead of having a day off, Marissa and Charlie were called to play in the relief band for Tammy Wynette. It was in this way that they had met, by having the same night off and being called to play in the relief bands. By agreement with the hotels and the Musicians' Union, each showroom orchestra was required have one day off per week. When several big-name singers were in town at the same time and using large string sections, no one sat at home; they sat in a relief band.

This night Marissa and Charlie found a booth in the coffee shop after the first show, where they went to have their between-show refreshments.

As soon as they were seated Marissa asked, "Where were you before the show started, Charlie? ... I was standing around waiting to go on when Tammy Wynette came over to talk to me. We had a nice chat. She told me what songs she's working on, and that she writes them while she's all curled up in the back seat of the bus they travel in. Then she told me about her little girl, who calls her every day to tell her what happened at school, or about her friends. Women like to talk to each other about their children. You know, when Joan Rivers comes in, she brings her five-year-old daughter Melissa, who is very tiny for her age, and Joan worries about that. Once, after I hadn't seen them for a while, I told Melissa I thought she had grown a whole lot, and they were so pleased to hear that."

"Gee, no big star ever comes up to talk with me. I'm jealous," said Charlie, pouting and sticking out his lower lip.

Marissa joshed back, "Over at your home base, Caesar's, they have only superstars, not human beings, that's why."

The waitress who knew Marissa came by and asked,

"The same salad, Marissa?"

"Yes Tricia, thanks."

Charlie ordered a sandwich and pie.

"So you get to talk to superstars, and on a first-name basis? Hmm-m, at Caesar's Palace, Frank Sinatra, Tony Bennett, Tom Jones, and Diana Ross are treated like royalty. On top of that, we have to address them as 'Mister' or 'Miss', and only when we have to ask a question."

"How elite," continued Marissa, raising her eyebrows. "I've been talking to little Janet Jackson every night this week. She gets kicked out of the two dressing rooms used by her brothers and has to use our restroom after each show. What a cute, pudgy nine-year-old, already with a lot of business sense, telling me their schedules and when they'll be back."

"Boy, you do draw headliners to you like flies, Hon."

'Hon'? Gee, that sounds good, but he must mean what the bees make. This man makes me feel good. I should invite him to coffee and donuts at my place.

Over the next few weeks Marissa went through her daily routine, practicing each day, then going about her daytime chores. At night between shows, she missed talking to Charlie, knowing that he had started his class and was studying hard. Several times she started to pick up the phone, but stopped each time.

Finally one morning, nervously summoning up enough courage, she did call. "Charlie, I know you're busy with classes, but how about coming over for brunch sometime?"

"Perfect timing. Uh, is today okay? How'd you know I needed a break?" Cheerfully, he said, "I'll be right over."

Imagine Marissa's surprise when Charlie showed up with his viola and a handful of music. "I felt like doing the

Mozart 'Sinfonia' today. You've played that, haven't you, hon?"

"Oh, sure, it's one of my favorites, especially the slow movement." Marissa's face brightened with this clever idea of Charlie's. "What a perfect catharsis to get the Strip music out of our systems. Playing this duet beats my cleanup exercises for the day."

Charlie took a couple of deep whiffs of the aromas coming from the kitchen. "Boy, it smells good in here and I'm getting hungry. Can I help you?" he asked, unloading his music and viola in the living room. His stomach was rumbling and his heart doing flip-flops.

"I'm putting lunch on the table now, Charlie, so if you can just set up the music stands for us for later, that'll help." *He must be awfully hungry the way he darts around.*

After placing the music on the stands and opening his viola case as fast as he could Charlie snuck closely behind Marissa, putting both hands gently on her shoulder. "I'm more hungry than I thought."

That gave Marissa goose bumps. "Here, everything's ready, let's sit down Charlie."

"Mmm. Hey, you're a good cook," Charlie said between bites after they started eating. You've got everything in this dish all bite-size—chicken, veggies and, oh, boy, tofu!"

"Next time, I'll have fried rice, or better yet, some home-style sushi. My grandmother up in San Francisco taught me how to make a lot of these stir-fries."

After a leisurely meal the two washed their hands before picking up their instruments in the living room. Marissa turned on the lamp for the music.

"I brought my good viola today. At work, I use an old French one that has a low voice."

"Oh, me too, I use one of dubious origin, but the sound carries well enough."

Looking closely at his viola, Marissa asked, "Charlie, isn't your viola a little small? I assumed it was full-size until I got this close now. That dark varnish, it's like a Bergonzi." "You're pretty well versed, hon. I'm surprised. Yes, this is about a 7/8th size viola, which may have been made by one of Carlo Bergonzi's sons. The Bergonzi family and the Stradivarius families lived next door to each other in Cremona in the 16th century, and I'm sure they exchanged ideas and techniques. Bergonzi did most of the repair work for the Strad workshop. Otherwise, he would have had time to make more fiddles. Anyway, whatever the provenances, I love this viola, and the size doesn't take away the full warm lower tones. I've tried other people's violas, and I find this size makes it easier for me to get around the instrument, especially for modern music.

All this impressed Marissa, who had been around antique collectors since childhood, and had heard many anecdotes about artists, patrons, collectors and imitators.

After tuning and warming up, Marissa was thrilled to find herself playing one of her favorite compositions, the Mozart *Sinfonia Concertante for Violin and Viola*. For her to be creating something this beautiful was fulfilling beyond expectation. Playing solo pieces was so different, whereas here, her melodies were backed by the viola's lower sounds, supporting her and enriching the blended harmonies. She was thrilled to feel the richness of sound the two instruments reverberated against her chest area.

During the reading she and Charlie stopped several times, with comments from him like, "When I echo that phrase you just played, back down," or pointing to her music, "play out here more, make it emphatic, Hon." Already, she was impressed with Charlie's humming or playing the orchestral parts when their solo parts were resting, so the music flowed as during a performance with no silence to break the spell.

Both musicians were worn out when they finished playing the first two movements. As new partners they needed to declare and blend their phrases that the music called for. They had to respond or "talk" to each other, and at the same time become acquainted with each other's style of playing. Both were pleased that their interpretations of Mozart were amicable, making the music flow effortlessly.

Taking a brief break, Charlie put his viola down and sighed. "Great to be playing our kind of music. You've had some fine training and your second movement was especially stirring and evocative. Hon, you should be playing with a string quartet or some chamber group."

"Sure, those jobs are scarce like hen's teeth, you know that. You certainly play well yourself, Charlie, and your sensitive playing allowed me to bring out the poignancy of Mozart."

"It's not often chamber musicians mesh this well on first readings," said Charlie. "I was in a pretty good group in San Diego, but it took months to sound like one unit. There were only six of us, but that job ended." *As well as a lukewarm friendship with a nice woman,* but he wasn't going to bring up that part of his past. "You know, the usual story: the funding stops, no renewal of contracts, and therefore no work."

While Marissa was putting her violin away he said, "Hon, you have a modern fiddle, don't you? It's been made by a master, I can tell, and its sound is even and is beautiful. Let me see it."

Handing it over to Charlie, Marissa said, "Yes, it's a Poggi. Ansaldo Poggi of Bologna made it in 1953. It's still quite new—what, twenty years old? And I'm nowhere near finished breaking it in," she said as she handed it to Charlie. "In Europe, his fiddles are in great demand because they're affordable and have the old master's sound. He made many models like this, after Stradivarius' 1714 violins."

Charlie picked up Marissa's bow. "What's this, a Tubbs bow? Hon, who advised you on these?"

"I had a good violin repairman in New York as a student at Juilliard, and I used to hang around his shop meeting the fiddlers who came in. I met a lot of famous soloists who used to come in and browse and talk shop and try out different instruments. I even got free advice whenever they wanted to hear me play on a violin they liked. Then they played on it. What fun, the back and forth of two different players on one instrument. Oh, boy, they always went for the Strads and Guarnerius's, which made me swoon. It was a treat to spend hours with good violinists in that shop."

Just as long as the swooning was when she was listening to fiddle music.

Charlie started playing on Marissa's violin, and was amazed at its sound. Being a violist rather than a violinist, he applied more pressure with his bow, as well as his male strength, and brought out the brilliance of sound that Marissa had not yet been able to produce. *I've got to learn to get that virtuouso sound,* she thought.

Charlie nodded approvingly. "Very nice, Hon. You've got good equipment for any important solo jobs, I see."

"I'm going to try using my bow like you do, Charlie. I like the sound you get out of my Poggi. In fact, when I practice every day, part of it is to clean up any bad habits I get into playing so loud for the show."

Charlie agreed, "Oh, me too. Some days, that's all the time I have, just to go through my scales and arpeggios. Yeah, we have to be on guard constantly to keep our playing pristine."

"What a battle, and no one realizes any of this... Don't you just envy people who love music, and blithely sing snatches of songs, as if all music were heaven-sent?"

"Yeah, they'll never know," said Charlie, shaking his head.

"Let's go through what we just played, and call it a day for music," he said.

"I was just going to suggest the same thing."

The second reading went much smoother, leaving them musically satisfied and feeling exalted by the music they had created together.

"Best to stop when we're ahead," said Marissa. "Let's finish the last movements another time."

Charlie helped with the dishes and stayed, making no move to go home.

"Come sit here next to me, Hon. What a great afternoon. I haven't had such a good time in ages."

"Same here. It's not always ... Oh, oh, ohh . . .!"

Charlie had moved closer, putting his arms around her and whispering, "Marissa, I've wanted to do this for ages. There's something so special about you. You're different from others." He loosened her black ponytail, gasping as her hair tumbled down over her shoulders, bringing out the tawny coloring on her flushed face. No more was said as they gradually abandoned their reserve, becoming totally absorbed in kissing and touching each other.

Many hours later, the two new lovers emerged from the shower somewhat in a daze.

"What's happening to us, Charlie?" whispered Marissa hoarsely.

"I've been enchanted by you ever since that night we sat by the swimming pool at the Flamingo Hotel."

"You, too? That's when I became interested in you, Charlie."

Holding her close, he said, "In the past, when I used to see you at other gigs, you seemed disinterested, so I didn't do

anything. If I'd only known then how much there is to you."
Charlie stayed over that night at Marissa's.

Chapter 4

That fall, even after the hectic summer season, there was no letup for casino workers with everyone working full time. Tourists poured into town each day, and on weekends the hotels were packed to capacity. Crowds of people would saunter along the Strip, squinting in the morning sunlight as they rubbernecked, enjoying the balmy sunshine. They were all eyes, taking pictures and noting the hotel marquees that flashed superstar names such as Frank Sinatra, Dean Martin, Ann Margret, Sonny and Cher, Elvis Presley, Tony Bennett, Glen Campbell, Herb Alpert, Tom Jones, and of course, Wayne Newton, the hometown superstar.

On such a day Marissa and Charlie were finally able to spend some free time together. They decided to go downtown. Downtown Las Vegas was what old-time residents and regular visitors considered the "real" Las Vegas.

They had been together the night before. When they awakened to a sunny morning, they showered together before having their coffee, looking forward to a carefree day.

Parking his car in a five-story garage downtown, they walked down one street, turning at the corner onto Fremont, and gaping like tourists at the crowd and storefront casinos that were lined up one next to another. With his arm around Marissa, Charlie told her, "I've not been down here in a while, and I'm always surprised that it's so different from the Strip."

Marissa was all eyes. "It has a small-town feel to it." Then she pointed, "That must be City Hall, and that white granite building across the street says "Federal Building"."

"Yeah, and in those modern buildings," Charlie pointed in another direction to 20-story windowed skyscrapers, "are the main branches of the banks in this town. Other floors are occupied by attorneys. Convenient location, close to the courthouse. "

Fremont Street had been the main thoroughfare of Las Vegas from the 1930s and was much narrower than the Strip. Its lineup of small storefront casinos was separated here and there by large hotels like Binion's Horseshoe and the Fremont Hotel, which Charlie and Marissa now passed.

When they came to The Golden Gate Hotel, they saw a big sign that read, "Shrimp Cocktail, 49 cents."

"Hey, Marissa, let's get a shrimp cocktail for an appetizer before lunch."

"Okay, you go ahead, and I'll just try a couple of yours. How can they do it for only 49 cents? Is it any good?"

Standing in line, Charlie said, "If they serve hundreds of people like this every day, they must have the stuff flown in regularly." Marissa watched as the people took their cups of tiny but plump shrimps to a service table to pick up their forks and napkins, and pour on the cocktail sauce. As they took their first bites to the satisfied sounds of "mmm-mm", it made her wish she had ordered one for herself, too.

Catching sight of her expression, Charlie gave her shoulder an affectionate squeeze as he popped one in her mouth. "Make you hungry?" he whispered seductively in her ear, really thinking *how I'd rather take bites of something of yours.*

With a quick sense of his double meaning, she flashed him a knowing look and blushed.

As they walked outside munching on the shrimp, Marissa stared again at her surroundings, where signs were flashing from each noisy open doorway to lure people into the small, store-sized casinos. Some down-and-outers, habitual gamblers, were playing penny slot machines. A brand new car was placed just inside the casino right next door. It had a bold sign aimed at making people believe how easy it was to win a car for 25 cents.

Marissa stopped and uttered, "It's like a carnival down here, isn't it?"

"Yeah, and kind 'a seedy, too. Look how narrow these streets are. And check out those old-fashioned business buildings, late 40s style with small windows," Charlie said pointing across the street as the two of them glanced up and around them. Bus and auto fumes as well as people bumping into the two of them only added to the unsavory atmosphere. "The county jail's around the corner," he said, sounding like a tourist guide.

Marissa gawked as she looked up and down the street. "Gee, I'd be afraid to work down here at night," she whispered, as she edged closer to Charlie. "Some of these people are creepy. I heard that Joe, the guitarist in the band, does weekend dance jobs at one of these joints, and he always brings back tales of drunken brawls—most of them involving women, yet.

"Hon, if you ever get called to work down here, use the valet parking service, and try to leave work with someone else. You'll eventually get called to play Wayne Newton at the Fremont Hotel as most of us have."

"Wow, I can see that there must be so much more of this town. Lots of offices and banks—and look," she pointed, "All those bail bond places! And what a combination, regular businesses that you see in any city's downtown, *plus* so many gambling joints. All co-existing like this. You know, I can see now that my life revolves around a couple of small circles: one around the Strip for work, the other around my neighborhood for errands to the bank, post office or shopping."

Stopping in front of The Mint, one of the larger casinos, they heard a barker yelling, "Fifty-cents per game, folks! Fifty-cents at the poker tables!" Charlie looked at his watch and said, "It's past noon now, so let's go to the buffet here. I heard it's good."

"Look, a dollar forty-nine lunch buffet here, Charlie, and only 99 cents down the street!", Marissa remarked in amazement, still taken in by the impressive street scene.

They walked through the spacious Mint Casino, passing gaming tables, roulette wheels and hundreds of slot machines with as many players, and rode the escalator to the second floor to a large dining room where aromas of food made them hungry.

"Not worth cooking at home, is it? Come," Charlie said, taking her hand gently with a protective air. "We'll check out all the entrees before serving ourselves."

After deciding on a lunch of salad, roast turkey, stuffing, and vegetables, they sat close together in a corner. They were happy that most of the diners were eating quietly and speaking softly, a welcome contrast to the rough crowd outside.

After a few bites, Marissa said "Yum! This is better than I can make at home. Did you see that man pile food onto his plate like he was building a mountain? Almost made me lose my appetite." She made a face and stuck out her tongue.

"Yeah, they know you can go back as many times as you want," said Charlie, savoring his salad. "I'll probably make several trips up there myself and end up eating as much as he does."

After their pumpkin pie dessert, Charlie paused to look at Marissa, eager to say what had really been on his mind. "Hon, what are you doing during the Christmas break? You know all the showrooms are closed during December."

"For goodness sake, Charlie, that's more than a month away. . . We-ell, I guess if I do anything, I'll go back home to see my folks. It'd be nice to be with them at Christmas."

"I'm asking now because free time's become scarce lately, and I want to make plans to enjoy every minute of my enforced vacation."

Good grief, this man is so methodical and organized, he wants to plan when and how he's going to have his fun. When he gets like this, it's hard to believe this is the same wild man in bed. She shivered slightly thinking about those moments.

"Hon, I was hoping we could make our token visits with our families, and after that, spend time together. Wouldn't you like that?"

She thought about it only a moment before saying, "Yes, that sounds perfect! How about San Francisco? My grandparents live there, and we could visit them. . . Or, do you want to come back here and explore other areas, like the time we went to Overton?"

It pleased Charlie that she had mentioned his work and his voice softened. "I'll be making enough of those trips during my studies, so let's go up to San Francisco," he said nudging his knee against hers. "I'd love to meet your grandparents, and you can show me around your old stomping grounds."

By the time they arrived at their respective homes for the Christmas holiday, they were both grateful to be far from their workplace for a change. Marissa had gone home to Monterey, while Charlie returned to Los Angeles. The distance of 500 miles gave them a chance to gain a better perspective of their friendship, but they missed each other sorely as all lovers do when apart.

Chapter 5

Meeting the Parents

So, you have a boyfriend, you say?" asked Mama anxiously. Papa was silently eating the peas from his salad with his chopsticks.

The dinner-hour conversation was usually full of the day's activities, but Marissa had known that sooner or later, she'd need to tell Mama and Papa about Charlie. Helping herself to more salad, Marissa continued, "Yes, Mama, I met Charlie at work. He plays viola and graduated from SC. He already has his Master's in American History and wants to go after his doctorate." Marissa wanted to build him up right away so she wouldn't be heaped with warnings about questionable characters. She hated this part of the visit.

Mama filled her dish with tofu and pork after finishing her salad. "Hmm. At least you season your food pretty well; in fact, it's a treat to have dinner ready for us after work."

My gosh—a compliment!

"Thanks, Mama. It was fun using the rice cooker since I don't have one. I wish other foods cooked automatically like that."

"Well," continued Mama, more interested in talking about Charlie. "If your friend is going back to school, how will he support himself? Next thing you know, you'll be living together with you paying his bills."

"Oh, Mama, he's too proud to do anything like that. Our music work in the hotels pays very well. Gee whiz, give me some credit for figuring out things like that. He's home for the holiday in Los Angeles talking to his parents too about us."

"What did you say his name is?"

"It's Charlie Lyons."

"And you say he's a nice person and serious?" Mama knew that this man was important to her daughter at this point in her life, and tried to be as affable as possible. "What do his parents do?" She was still apprehensive and wondered if she was asking too many questions.

"His father's a civil engineer. He got his degree under the G.I. Bill of Rights like you did, Papa. They live in LA, he travels a lot as a consultant, and his mother works at an art gallery in the Wilshire District, I'm not too sure about details."

Mama and Papa nodded approvingly.

"Just as long as you don't get mixed up with those hotel people and gamblers."

"Oh, them! All they go after is lots of cash to buy flashy things so they can show off and feel superior."

The family ate without further conversation. Marissa's parents had had a busy day, Mama at a gift shop, and Papa as an instructor at the Defense Language School. He was teaching the same things he had studied when he went to Camp Savage in Minnesota during the war. His students were preparing to become interpreters in the diplomatic services. Not only did they need to know the Japanese language well, they also needed to know the subtleties of behavior as well as other concerns related to the work. Besides the reading, writing, calligraphy and correct pronunciations, there were also the proper mannerisms of when to nod, bow, or pause. Marissa was always fascinated by these differences in Japanese and American cultures, and was glad she didn't have to remember to kowtow to her superiors all the time.

The next day, Charlie phoned from his parent's home in Los Angeles. After whispering a few sweet nothings to Marissa, he said softly, "Boy, do I miss you, hon."

A delicious shiver ran through Marissa as his deep

masculine voice reminded her of their private moments. "Oh, Charlie, I can't stand being away from you. The good news is that when I told my folks about us, they didn't get hostile and find everything wrong with what I'm doing. Even without meeting you, they think you sound okay. It might be a good idea to come here, meet them, and after that, the two of us can drive up to San Francisco and have a little fun."

"I'd thought of that, too," said Charlie enthusiastically, "But first, let me tell you something *sensational* that's happened here! I told my folks about you, and they seemed to take it gracefully, so I'm sure we won't have troubles there." He was getting breathless as he continued, "But listen to this, Hon ... Mom's brother died recently. I may have told you that. Anyway, he was a bachelor and left her a nice inheritance, and he also mentioned me in his will. It's like a miracle. Do you know what this means? I can go on with my studies without worrying about bills all the time. I'll tell you more when we see each other. In fact, this bequest brings about some legal stuff I have to do, so after visiting you, I'll need to go to a lawyer in Las Vegas right away. We'll have to make plans for San Francisco some other time."

Charlie sat close to Marissa on the couch, facing her parents who were trying to put him at ease by passing around photo albums of Marissa as a child.

"We took these pictures on her birthdays and on Girls' Day, which is in March. See, here's one where we dressed her in a red kimono when she was five years old," said Mama proudly.

"She looks like a little doll," said Charlie. He was nervous, and hoped for approval from her parents by bowing a lot, as he remembered Japanese friends doing when they came to visit his parents.

Marissa was amazed that her parents were accepting Charlie, as he told them of his deep interest in history—particularly American history—which was sparked by one of his teachers in high school. He explained that he had always loved going to the library and checking out history books. He then mentioned that his mother played piano and how he loved sitting on the floor under the grand piano when she used to practice. She had started him on piano, but when violinists came to play sonatas with her, he fell in love with the stringed instrument sound.

"So, I've grown up with music around me, and can't imagine living without it."

Mama stood up, saying, "It makes a difference when one has grown up with music. I played piano a little, and sometimes accompanied Marissa when she finished learning a new piece. I hear that you play very well, Charlie." As she headed for the kitchen, to keep him at ease she added, "I've got a roast in the oven that smells like dinner's almost ready!"

Papa and Charlie started talking politics, at which point Marissa said she would go help Mama with dinner. The two men enjoyed each other's company, and Charlie was anxious to bring up his work in college. "Sir," he began respectfully, "At one point in our California history classes we learned how badly the Chinese and Japanese workers were treated when they first came to this country. I'm ashamed to say that this state has not been good to either people, and I was horrified when we studied about the evacuation of thousands of Japanese Americans right after Pearl Harbor. And now I am especially so, after meeting Marissa and learning that you underwent that unfair experience. I wanted to talk to you about it. Do you mind? Marissa doesn't seem to know much about those years before she was born, and if it doesn't bother you, uhhh, someday, I'd appreciate hearing about it from you." It had taken all of Charlie's nerve to broach this subject.

"To tell the truth," Papa said, "My wife and I never speak about it anymore, but something on that grand a scale needs to be brought out in the open, discussed, and recorded. . . objectively, if possible. The emotions are buried within us. Yes, I've been wanting to do something about it, but keep procrastinating. As a matter of fact, I'm glad you brought it up, and you're pretty much the perfect person to share my side of the story with. Give me a little time, and I'll get into my trunk sometime soon, and get a story together for you. I managed to save my journal from my college days. As you mentioned, Marissa knows very little about those years. We never wanted her to be hurt as we were, and it's as if we simply wished the memory of those years away."

Charlie was overwhelmed with the old man's offer. It was like being promised a treasure. "Sir, as a historian, I want you to know that what you are offering is truly a wonderful gift. Thank you."

"Now, now, don't go around 'sir-ing' me, Charlie. You're the one who has a master's, which I don't have, so I should call you 'sir.' Just call me George."

In the kitchen, Mama told Marissa, "Papa and I like your friend very much. We can tell he is a fine young man of good character. Try to be worthy of him and develop a friendship that will last your lifetime. I can see how compatible you are. Work at it. You know, sometimes it's not going to be easy, but I think you'll find happiness with each other."

Marissa considered this to be a blessing, and was beaming all during the leisurely dinner, especially with her usually dour Papa being so convivial with Charlie. The young couple was relieved to have survived the trials of this first meeting.

◆

Chapter 6

Charlie had an appointment back in Las Vegas, and left right after visiting Marissa and meeting her parents. Marissa stayed on for a few days, which greatly pleased her parents who missed their only child. She felt rather lonely coming back to her hometown to find that most of her classmates had found jobs in larger cities and moved away. Boredom set in, with only so much she could do after browsing in all the gift shops in Carmel and Steinbeck's Cannery Row, lovely as they were. She was able to have dinner ready for her parents when they came home tired after each day's work, and was happy that it delighted them.

One evening, almost finished with dinner, her mother suddenly declared, "I've never heard of such outrageous working hours. Couldn't you find a job with regular hours like everyone else? And look at the clothes you're wearing—humph, such loud colors. What kind of people do you associate with when you're out all hours of the night?"

Her dad was quiet, sipping his favorite Sapporo beer that Marissa had poured for him as soon as he sat down. He was happy that his little family was together, in spite of the frequent mother-daughter bickering.

Marissa pulled her blouse out in front of her, saying impatiently, "Mama, I'm living in the desert now, and the sun's so bright, we need colorful clothes like this. That's why Van Gogh used brilliant colors when he lived in Arles. You always liked his paintings. Anyway, the grays and navy blues you wear around here would make me look like I'm dying over in Vegas, so why not wear my favorite colors—oranges, pinks and purples?

Oh, cripes, by the looks of her, I can see more lectures coming up. I'd better get this in: "Mama, tourists go to Las

Vegas to have a good time, and hundreds of them stay up way past midnight. Okay, so they get wild with those free drinks, but don't think that means that I go partying with them. I work there and need to keep a sensible daily schedule. What more do you want? You think of nothing but work, work, work, but normal people take time out, go on vacations and do something different and have fun."

"Yes, but you get up so late every morning."

Marissa knew it was hopeless to continue with an old-fashioned mind-set like that. *Thank God, I'm not living at home anymore.*

The following day, Marissa had lunch with a school friend who had recently opened a boutique shop in Carmel. Carol was eager to hear all about Las Vegas. She was in her early thirties and was excited and fascinated by the glamour surrounding Marissa's work. Thankfully, she was all ears, and made Marissa feel that her lifestyle was wonderful and to be envied.

"Yeah it's great to be playing in a band for all those big-name stars," Marissa was explaining to her. "You'd be surprised what regular people they are backstage. Some are quite friendly with us. In fact, it's their managers who are the impossible ones; they're so taken with their positions, you'd think *they* were the famous household names. Anyway, like clockwork, singers come in for two weeks at a time, which is long enough for them to recognize and greet us in the hallways. Our dressing rooms are all pretty close together on one floor. We play two shows a night: the dinner show first, and the one at midnight with cocktails. When the stars are finished with their run, they give us a party on closing night."

"Oh, really, a party every two weeks? Goll-lee, what a life, Marissa!" Carol exclaimed excitedly. "What kind of food do they serve?"

"They always have a giant bowl of shrimp cocktails right in the center of the main table, and on a couple of other tables are great finger foods like rumaki, cold cuts so we can make Dagwoods, and cheeses we never see in grocery stores, plus lots of beer and wines."

This was too much for Carol, who shrieked, "Booze, too! During working hours?"

"Oh sure, and you should hear some of the final shows after these parties where we barely make it onstage for the last curtain call. That's when, in their semi-sober state, if the star who'd been partying with us forgets the song, the trumpet player blares out the song like he's the soloist so he can get everyone back together again. I've looked out in the audience at those times, and not a single person out there notices anything has gone amiss because it all happens so fast. Also, don't forget, those people sitting out there have been into plenty of free cocktails themselves, so they're having the time of their lives."

"How absolutely fascinating to be working with geniuses." Carol was beside herself listening to these behind-the-scenes stories of what she considered a fantastic way to earn a living.

Oh, thank goodness, Carol is all ears and can take these tales in stride. In fact, she finds this so exciting it's heartening, making me feel as if what I'm doing is not so wrong after all.

Leaning forward, Carol asked eagerly, "Have you ever played for Sonny and Cher? Their TV program is my favorite!"

"Why sure, many times. Cher is a marvelous singer and dancer. I swear, some of the jokes and bantering with Sonny are so off the cuff, the two of them even surprise themselves that what they've just said came off so wittily." Marissa's eyebrows then went up and down like Groucho's as she said, "And Carol, you should see the slinky dresses she wears—more sexy than you'd ever see on TV!"

Ever the devoted TV watcher and *People* magazine reader, Carol asked, "Do you hear rumors about them divorcing?"

"Oh, we don't believe half of those things, and frankly, most of us don't care about their private lives. There's so much fake publicity about them, we ignore much of it."

After a pause, now that she had Carol in an eager listening mood, Marissa said thoughtfully, "You know who puts on a pretty good show is Tony Orlando."

"Why him?"

"Besides his own hit songs like 'Tie a Yellow Ribbon,' 'Candida,' and 'Knock Three Times,' as well as a show favorite, 'Hey, Jude,' he has a way of getting his audience all worked up. He could have them singing hymns, and you'd think you were at an outdoor Sunday revival service with people being totally carried away ... And another one who has that kind of charisma is Mac Davis. He grew up in Texas around Gospel singers. Once, his whole family was invited to the celebration at a Negro church that his Dad had rebuilt, gratis, following a hurricane. Mac and Tony both have the ability to touch their audiences on a very personal level, and the whole showroom rocks when they get their roused up audience all singing together."

"Wow, Marissa, you know so much about these famous stars." Carol's eyes were shining bright. "It sounds like you go to parties and get to be friends with famous stars, and you do this every night. How cool!" Carol's voice was reaching a higher pitch with every little anecdote Marissa shared with her.

"Carol," said Marissa patiently in a serious tone of voice, "I get a chance to watch each show over a two-week period without interruptions; most of us learn our parts well enough after two or three days, and then we manage to take in all the details of the production. I've finally figured out what's important. It's the creative crew in the background that the audience never sees: a good director, a good choreographer, and a good musical arranger are the backbone of a show. Oh, yes, the costume director, too. You'd be surprised how closely women in the audience scrutinize the costumes. I hear them talking in the coffee shop after the shows, and they go over every little detail of what the performers were wearing."

"Geez, you make it sound like a business, Marissa."

"You – bet – it - is! We all work our buns off so the audience can sit out there, relax, be entertained, and forget all about their ho-hum daily routines. We make it seem easy and fun, like it just happens naturally, but believe me, a lot of thought goes into every moment of a show."

"You're so lucky to be in show biz, Marissa. Not your ordinary nine-to-five, is it? Well, let me ask you, since I'm in the clothing business, whose costumes do you like?"

Leaning her head sideways, Marissa thought for a moment before saying, "I'm most impressed with Dionne Warwick's *gorgeous* gowns. She comes onstage with beautifully textured gowns with rich color combinations you never see anywhere else. Did you know that Marlene Dietrich took her under her wing after Burt Bacharach introduced them? Burt started out in show biz as Dietrich's pianist. Anyway, Dietrich told her own designer in Paris to outfit Dionne after she heard Dionne sing Burt's songs. After that, Dionne's always had an outstanding stage wardrobe … And since you asked about costumes, there are singers like Helen Reddy or Vikki Carr, on the other hand, who don't seem to care so much about wearing flashy ones or moving their bodies seductively. But there are plenty of loyal fans who think their idols can do no wrong and come in droves to hear their favorite tunes being sung live by their favorite singers. And you should see them singing along with the star, totally enraptured."

After a pause, Marissa giggled when another thought came to her. "Crystal Gayle comes in wearing beautiful filmy gowns, and she appears to float around like a nymph with her dream-like movements and graceful body swaying when she's singing. Her long dark hair reaches down to her knees, and the guys in the band have their tongues hanging out. We girls watch them amusedly when they squeeze their knees together, frowning and playing their horns as if nothing was bothering them," she chortled, making Carol laugh gleefully.

"Honestly, what little devils you girls are! I just love hearing about your work, Marissa. I want you to come to my shop some time because I just put in a new line of accessories I'd like to give you—you know, like scarves and costume jewelry. Do you wear any when you work?"

"Oh, absolutely. With our required black outfits, we like to at least indulge ourselves with sparkly rings and touches of color in our pendants or hair ornaments."

"I have them all, so be sure to drop by."

"Okay, I will. I've become a little more clothes-conscious since I started working in Vegas. You can teach me about color schemes, accessories and all that stuff that I've never paid attention to before. I'll come by your shop tomorrow. Gee thanks, Carol, for helping me and also for listening and making me feel that my work is worth something. You should hear Mama—she's not with it at all and just doesn't understand."

They hugged and said their goodbyes, Carol with stars in her eyes, stepping sprightly down the cobblestone sidewalk back to her shop, and Marissa walking slowly back to her car to go home and start dinner for her folks. She missed Charlie even more after talking so much about show biz to Carol. It suddenly occurred to her that she hadn't mentioned him at all during their lunch because she was so busy talking about her work—in Las Vegas of all places!

But that's where she had found the most important man in her life.

Chapter 7

Oo-oo, this place is so much bigger than I'd expected," cooed Marissa gleefully as she stood enraptured in the center of the spacious living room of their new apartment. Going over to the couch, she patted it, "This, and your easy chair already gives the room a settled feel."

Nodding enthusiastically, Charlie's head bobbed around as he inspected the spaciousness... "Tall ceiling, and the windows well-placed to let in lots of light."

Hurrying to the kitchen doorway, Marissa smiled as she looked in.

"And how I love this kitchen, dear. It's family-sized with a large fridge so we won't keep running out of food. And look, a dishwasher! No more dirty dishes piling up in the sink, ever." A table and four matching chairs were invitingly placed for unhurried meals. She was grateful that, from time to time, Charlie had managed to bring old pieces of his family's furniture from Los Angeles. It dawned on her that her home in Monterey was sparsely furnished with only the basic necessities, mainly because her parents had returned there with only a few suitcases of clothes, much the same way that they were forced to leave California after Pearl Harbor. Household goods were not readily available in the mid-forties, the rebuilding period after wartime shortages, and she remembered the few times when buying new pieces of furniture was a big event during her childhood.

Charlie was outside the bathroom, pointing in, "Don't forget, we have this and another one, so we can each take showers at the same time before going to work." She hurried down the hallway to join him, her smile wider than ever. "You know, you were right about us moving in together. There's plenty of space so we can concentrate on our work and not worry about getting in each other's way."

They went back to the living room in a cheerful mood and lay down on the beige-carpeted floor, on oversized cushions. Charlie and a student from school had carted the heavy things from the car to the new apartment. He was ready to call it a day. He stretched out his arms and legs, gave a big sigh, and said in a pleased tone of voice, "Whew, I'm glad we're finally moved in! We'll rearrange all that stuff later, if necessary."

Marissa, now relaxed, asked languidly, "Do you realize how much your uncle's generosity is going to help us? You can take on more classes and be able to go to the Reno campus to their archives. Mainly, you won't have financial worries and can concentrate on getting your doctorate."

"Yup, that was some unexpected surprise," Charlie said brightly. "You're right, I will take on two more classes, and feel free to run up to Reno or drive to old mining towns and look for old-timers drifting about to interview them."

"That all sound good." Marissa rambled on, "I'll just keep on with all the shows that I get called for. Next week, Sinatra is switching to our hotel—don't know why he's leaving Caesar's. I hear that our management is anxious about having everything just right, especially for his wife Barbara. Can you imagine, she brings her own set of sheets for their odd-sized beds in Hollywood, and already the hotel is scrambling around ordering special beds built for her sheets."

"You gotta be kidding! Now, I've heard everything. One thing, though," Charlie added, "you'll like playing his show. He has the best arrangers in the business where a band can't help but sound good, and the men who travel with him are just super. He's mellowing and is easier to work for. His son, Frank Junior, says that when playing most cities where they add local players, they can hardly wait to come here where they can be sure that our musicians play well enough to suit his dad. It makes him comfortable while performing. " With that, he closed his eyes and put his arms around Marissa as both glided noiselessly into a little cat nap.

Sinatra rehearsal: Seated onstage, the band members were unusually well-behaved and somber. After all, they were going to be rehearsing with Frank Sinatra for the first time this morning at 11 o'clock. He had just signed up with this hotel after ten years' headlining across the street at Caesar's. The players were well aware of Sinatra's popularity and his power in the music business. To top it off, he knew what sounds he wanted from a band, even if he didn't know the theories of orchestration. He simply had that innate gift.

Forty musicians, about a third of them women, were seated stadium-style, looking over their folders containing the music they would be playing for the next two weeks. The curtain was up, and the busboys were cleaning the showroom, collecting glasses and plates left from last night's show. They always worked quickly because as soon as Sinatra arrived, they had to leave. For other stars, they remained and kept on clattering the dishes, even vacuuming during a rehearsal.

"Say, look at this, Sam," said Marissa to her stand partner. She was in the large string sections of eighteen players, and was leafing through the line-up. She pulled out a worn manuscript.

"Huh, what? asked Sam who was warming up on his violin with a mute on. He was one of those players who liked to go over scales and arpeggios before starting rehearsals, while Marissa simply picked up her violin and felt ready to go. On the other side of the bandstand, a trumpet player also had on his mute and was doing sustained notes, and a clarinetist and a flutist were going over the same spot in harmony. Sam stopped and looked at the music that Marissa pulled out. "That's a pretty messy copy," he commented. "It's his big hit from years ago, 'Witchcraft.' You'll like it. Just be careful in the beginning, right here," he said, pointing to the spot with his bow.

"I've made a lot of recordings in Hollywood with stars like Sinatra, and remember some of the places one needs to play carefully at first."

"Gee, Sam, I'm lucky to be sitting with you with all your long experience in this business." Marissa was nervous because she had heard how demanding Sinatra was musically. Tommy Dorsey was the young Sinatra's strict taskmaster back in the '40's when they toured the country.

The conductor for this show, Billy Mays, a good-natured rotund man, was standing at the podium, studying his score.

Sinatra came onstage wearing a red baseball cap, but Marissa did not recognize him at first. He had come in with a couple of other men, probably Jilly and his henchmen. Sinatra greeted the conductor, then nodded to his pianist, Bill Miller, and scanned the bandstand, waving to Irv Cotter, his drummer, then greeted the band. "Good morning, everyone."

The busboys quickly left the showroom. The only people remaining were Sinatra's staff, who were scattered at various points for this first appearance in a different hotel.

Billy raised his baton and said to the band, "Good morning .... Let's start with the first number, please, "I've Got the World On a String."

While the band played the introduction, Sinatra looked at the score on his own stand and listened to this new band. He nodded approvingly as he looked around at the players. He had been cautioned at the other hotel that this band was not up to his standards, so he was doubly pleased to hear the excellent sounds, confirming his belief that there are fine players everywhere. The sounds were different, but the unmistakably fine musicianship of these players came through.

"Very good, guys, let's do the next one, "Come Fly With Me."

Soon, it was like any other rehearsal with the band going through more hits, such as: "All The Way," "Close To You," "Guess I'll Hang Out My Tears To Dry," and "Come Dance With Me." Forty-five minutes had gone by, and the band manager yelled, "Break!"

Everyone gave a sigh of relief that this part of the rehearsal finished without any catastrophe. The musicians stood up to shake off the nervous tension, some going outside for a cigarette, while others rushed to the little room where there was coffee and Danish for them. Onstage, electricians, sound engineers came on, busily dragging power lines, lighting men climbing 12-foot ladders with lamps, or the sound men adjusting microphones in the bleachers.

Sinatra's bass player who had been playing next to Marissa smiled and complimented her as she stood up to leave. "You and your partner sound very good."

Marissa never expected this and became flustered. "Oh, really? Uh, gee thanks…You mean you can hear us over the whole band?"

"Sure, you're sitting right next to me." Peering at Sam, he asked, "You've been in some of the recording sessions down in LA, haven't you?"

This pleased Sam, who said, "Yes, I recognized you when you came in. I did live in LA and played in a lot of recording dates, but I decided to move here because the schedule suits me better."

"I'm happy myself, playing and traveling with Sinatra all over the world."

When everyone returned from the break, Sinatra asked for "The Lady Is A Tramp." By now, the band was sufficiently warmed up, fully awake and swinging. Sinatra was pleased and said, "We need a little coda on this tune. The folks out there"—pointing to the showroom—"just won't stop clapping. So, Bill, where's a good spot to go back to for a mini-coda?"

Bill Miller, the pianist flipped his music back a few pages and said, "We did the last 32 bars from letter R. That always worked out best."

While the musicians hurriedly penciled in a note in their music, Sinatra grinned mischievously and said, "Hey, guys, look at Bill. He's so white, he's moon-glowed, spends all his time outside at night." Hee-haws from the men who slapped their thighs with raucous laughter. Bill took this good-naturedly, and waved his right hand at them, while at knee level, his left hand middle finger was furiously pumping up and down.

The second day's rehearsal went as well and by the end of the second hour, everyone was getting anxious to be dismissed. After all, this was opening night to a packed house and they wanted to go on feeling and looking bright and fresh. Sinatra and his staff came onstage, said a few words to each other, then Sinatra said, "Thank you, everyone, we'll see you tonight …. Oh, by the way, ladies," he looked at the women string players, "Do me a favor, would you? Please wear outfits that are NOT black."

Gasps of surprise from the women. Sinatra continued, "Christ, when I was growing up, every one of my aunts and their friends, when they became widowed, wore black for the rest of their lives. I got so sick of being surrounded by women in black, I couldn't stand it. You pretty ladies, come in wearing colorful outfits, okay? Just go through your closets, and I'm sure you'll find something suitable. Thanks.

"Darn it, I just splurged on a new black dress especially for this show …."

"Oh, my goodness, I don't have any dressy outfits with nice color…"

"My mother-in-law gave me an awful green dress, but it's color. Boy, when she hears that I wore it to play on opening night for a Frank Sinatra show, she'll be bragging about it forever …."

With that, the band hurried home.

Thankfully, after a successful opening night, Sinatra's show continued to please the packed house for the rest of the two-week run. This was the first time in a Strip showroom that women wore non-black evening clothes, much to their delight, and the envy of all the other women playing in the showroom bands.

The week before Christmas, rehearsals and phone calls began stirring things up in the newly settled household as the symphony prepared for the Bach "Christmas Oratorio" concert with rehearsals for small orchestra and large chorus. Charlie got a call to do a New Year's Eve show for Don Rickles, while Marissa was asked to do Wayne Newton. "Wayne won't want to get off, and his fans won't let him, so I landed a long show." Charlie told her knowingly, "You'll get plenty of overtime… Just be careful when you're driving home."

Each day, their mailbox was crammed with Christmas cards from friends scattered around the country. One day, Charlie yelled "Mail call!" as he walked in the front door, arms loaded with red and green envelopes along with two large packages.

Marissa had just finished cleaning up the kitchen from breakfast, and came running. "All that for us? My, aren't we the popular ones. Say, these packages are from my parents. Good thing we sent them and your folks their presents last week.

Here, you open this one, and I'll open this---it feels like a book."

"Oh boy, look Hon ... tapes, six of them: a couple of late Beethovens, one Rubenstein doing Chopin Nocturnes, Johann Strauss Waltzes, one Primrose, and one Heifetz. Great additions to our collection. . . Wait, here's more, but these are gift-wrapped, so we'll wait until Christmas Eve."

Marissa opened the other package, and pulled out a binder that was filled with pages and pages of what looked like a long story. She sat very still as she read a single page letter in longhand from her father:

Dear Marissa and Charlie,

Well, I went and got out my diary and started going through it. After several read-throughs, I knew that a whole bunch of scribbled notes or a list of key words wasn't going to make sense to anyone but me, so after mulling over it, decided to become a storyteller and set my wartime experiences down as a chronicle of what it was like after the attack on Pearl Harbor. At first, it was like writing a composition for an English class, but as I kept on with each new chapter, I was surprised by how much I enjoyed writing. It sure takes a different kind of skill, this storytelling, and I began to feel like a different person after each session at the typewriter. I can assure you that every incident is as true and accurate as I recall them, and the entire contents in the binder are 'from the horse's mouth'---(from the beast that lived in the stall where your mother and her parents lived for six months.)

Read through this first part and let me know if you get a feel of what it was like for me when I was your age. I'm also hoping that this kind of record can sit on your shelves as something to keep as part of our family history. I'll keep adding new chapters until I've covered the whole period of World War II. *Love, Papa*

Marissa and Charlie, here's my story that begins on Pearl Harbor Day, December 7, 1941.

◈

PART 2 SUBITO

An Intimate Look at Internment After Pearl Harbor

Chapter 8

Thank goodness it's Sunday. Here, in my room at the boarding house in Berkeley, I can laze around for an hour before starting to cram for this week's finals. I try to reassure myself that a rested brain can get me through exams better. I can hear the other students upstairs moving around quietly as they start their day. I usually go home to San Francisco on weekends to stretch out and eat Mom's cooking, but not today. Speaking of food, I'm getting hungry. Heck, it's almost eleven o'clock. Better get some coffee into me and start studying.

"I'll Never Smile Again" is coming from the radio down the hall. It must be Tommy already up and studying in his room. Tommy Miyamoto has been my best friend since we were kids. . . Dang, I wish I were a musician, but, here I am in college, studying to be a biologist. If everything goes according to schedule we'll become seniors next year, and when we graduate we'll have good jobs. I want to make my parents happy and proud. They've worked so hard all these years. I've always felt I owed it to them to make their dream come true—a son with a college degree. I want to go into research.

Wonder what openings there are for us Japanese. If I go back East to another college, I'll get better connections to labs. I want to be where there's not the prejudice against Orientals that's rife in California. Sometimes, I get tired of having to be not simply good, but to be far superior to others to be granted average rewards.

The war news is not good, and I'm concerned how the Nazis have the upper hand in Europe and North Africa. They're in Russia, too. And the horrors in Poland, where they're herding Jews into concentration camps and killing them off. Ugh, cruel s.o.b's.

Italian, German and Japanese residents in the U.S. are under surveillance, and the government has frozen large bank accounts of these people with money whose loyalties are questionable. For them, it's really war already. At home, Mom and Pop are nervous wrecks, especially after that last letter from relatives in Japan that said we will be at war against each other any day now. My folks tell me not to worry, just concentrate on my studies and get the degree so I can get started in my chosen profession.

"Hey, George, come here quick!" yelled Tommy, sounding panic stricken as he turned his radio up full blast.

I ran down the hall to his room where the radio announcer was shouting, "The Japs have attacked Hickam Field in Pearl Harbor!" Tommy looked stunned and his face was drained of color. The announcer continued, "Four hundred Japanese planes flew in and bombed Pearl Harbor. U.S. Navy warships were attacked and sunk."

"JAPAN'S ATTACKED US. . . IN HAWAII! WE'RE AT WAR NOW!" shouted Tommy.

Feeling lightheaded, I collapsed onto his bed. "HO-LY KE-RISTE! It's finally happened, huh? Just like our relatives in Japan said it would." Knowing that I'd have to calm myself to take some action, I kept my voice low and tried to sound controlled. "Listen, Tommy. Life isn't going to be the same again . . . ever. We gotta be careful now." Feeling like a trapped animal, I got up and ran back to my room shouting, "Pack up quickly. I'm driving home right now, before the cops start stopping any movement on the Bay Bridge or in the city."

Tommy and I threw our books and clothes together and beat it out of Berkeley in my Chevy jalopy. Through the shock, confusion and heavy traffic, we held our breaths and got home over the Bay Bridge to Japantown in San Francisco by early afternoon. Most of the people in the streets along the way hadn't heard of the attack yet, and we managed to drive home unnoticed.

Once in the house, we kept the radio on for the rest of the day. Even though Mom and Pop were relieved to see me, they scrambled about the house, a large, rented one, soberly gathering all the papers they thought were important. Wearing serous expressions, they crammed immigration papers from 25 years ago, and all our birth certificates, including mine and my younger sister's and kid brother's into the drawers of their steamer trunk. They even put in vaccination papers and school records and rent receipts. Our large stack of photos was cut down to a handful. Some boxes were there, too, but I don't know what was in them.

Being the big brother, I tried to explain to Yone, my thirteen year-old sister, and my kid brother, Hiro, who was nine, the best way I could about current events, politics and war. Poor kids, they didn't know what it was all about, only sensed there was trouble in the grown-up world. I tried to hide any fears and distracted them by going to the closet to take out the Monopoly game box. I told them it was better to stay indoors, even if it was a beautiful, sunny afternoon. Mom and Pop talked in low voices as they pulled out papers from drawers and closets, making a pile in the kitchen.

Toward suppertime, the radio announcer said there were more attacks on Pearl Harbor, with the Islands on high alert. One local radio station run by a liberal owner proclaimed, "Prior to the bombings, senior commanders in Hawaii concluded there was no reason to believe attacks were imminent, leaving planes parked wingtip to wingtip on airfields, anti-aircraft guns unmanned with ammunition boxes kept locked, and no torpedo nets protecting the fleet anchorage. Being a Sunday, many officers and crewmen were caught ashore spending a leisurely day off."

Mom and Pop stayed busy gathering all the letters and

photos they thought best to burn, and then waited until dark to make a small fire in our backyard. We had calendar pictures of the Japanese Royal Family, as did most of the Japanese immigrants who lived all over California. Those went into the pile, too. It was not that our family was loyal to Japan or their Emperor. My parents were always telling us kids how extremely grateful we should be to live in America, and how the law protected us so we were able to grow up and get good schooling, education being of utmost importance to them. They clung to the sense that they were Japanese, with the Royal Family a symbol of respect, a part of their heritage, but not due their loyalty. Here, in this new land, they felt contempt from many Americans around them. However, living in a cosmopolitan city, they were acquainted with a few enlightened people who were friendly toward us. They were the ones who loved Oriental arts and regarded us in a different light.

However, most Japanese people in rural communities were embittered and humiliated by callow treatment from the white farmers around them. Who can blame those Japanese living on farms if they were pro-Japan, even if they had been looked down as lowly peasants back home? What a sad situation for them that they were so badly treated in their adopted country as well.

After a restless night, the first news in the morning was that the United States and Britain had declared war on Japan. We heard over and over about the attack on Pearl Harbor, what a sneak attack the Japs pulled on us, and about the large number of casualties, those wounded or killed, along with names of the ships that were sunk. A lot of the officers were guys my age or a little older, and I might have gone to school with them. Each time I heard the news, I'd feel, this must be a bad dream, and at any moment, I'd wake up to find everything back to normal.

There was an immediate outcry up and down California to round up all the Japs and send them back to Japan, never mind that most of us were born here, and had never been out of this country. We were afraid to go outside to the stores, even for our groceries, but I told Mom I would get enough stuff for the next few days. Everyone tried to stick to his routine.

When I called the college, Tommy and I were advised to go back to take our finals. Within the next week, we drove nervously back to Berkeley. Without incident, we passed our exams. At least, our semester's work didn't go to waste, and we had those credits on our record. Of course, we didn't register for any more classes. Heck, we might even be called up for army duty. All the guys we knew were talking about it. Some of our Caucasian classmates had volunteered for duty and would leave after the holidays.

At the dean's office they told Tommy and me to contact the WCCA, Wartime Civilian Control Agency, a newly created department that was in charge of 'rounding' up all the Japanese residents of California, Oregon and Washington state. We were also advised to keep this to ourselves. It hit me that it was true that we were going to be sent away from our homes, and I worried about where they were going to send us.

At the boarding house in Berkeley we reluctantly packed all our belongings, gave away most of our books, said goodbye to the guys we liked the most, and drove back to San Francisco. How I was going to miss my car that I'd saved money for and fixed over and over. I was so fond of it, like it was a pet. Sadly, I knew that I'd have to give it up, plus this way of life that I had begun to enjoy, the new friends I'd made in the academic atmosphere, feeling more and more a part of mainstream America. It was sad to have to say good-bye to our new friends. Several guys and a girl gave us their home addresses, promising to keep in touch. Others politely wished us well, but were too timid to display further concern for us.

At home, Japantown was in an uproar, in a whirlpool of panic and rumors. The most persistent one was that we were going to be sent inland, away from the coast. Our radios were later confiscated, as well as our Brownie cameras. For God's sake, what harm could we do with a Philco table model radio, or a simple camera that children used?

For Japanese businessmen it was a traumatic nightmare. Every bit of effort they had sunk into their life's work was being destroyed. Hardly anyone owned homes. Our immigrant parents were denied citizenship, and without it, were not able to own real estate. Some wise folk, however, purchased houses or farmland in their American children's names, those who had the means to do so. In the farm country, this was more prevalent, with young Japanese Americans owning thousands of acres of undeveloped land.

Within a month, true to what the college advisor told us, the Wartime Civilian Control Agency (WCCA) was officially formed. It was to coordinate the removal of all Japanese people from the three west coast states, Washington, Oregon and California.

This was the office Tommy, I, and several other Japanese American students at Cal were told to contact to help coordinate this massive move. There were a handful of older men from the Japantown community that were relied upon for their mature negotiating skills. Around Easter, four months after Pearl Harbor, we all gathered in this government office downtown for orientation to help run the Assembly centers. We were necessary employees; otherwise, we would never have been hired by an American government agency. We were treated with distrust, but since we were bilingual we could facilitate the evacuation by giving information and orders to the older folk before the ouster.

The Agency had located and set up 17 assembly centers in California. These sites were formerly migrant workers' camps, fair grounds, race tracks and CCC camps. They enclosed these grounds with barbed wire fences and had armed military police patrolling the perimeter. Existing structures were adapted for use as offices, infirmaries, warehouses, and mess halls. At the racetracks, all stables were cleaned out for living quarters for small families. When it was determined that more housing was necessary, barracks-type buildings were hastily built for larger families. Each barrack contained six 26X20 rooms. The exterior was covered with one-ply roofing paper for insulation. Each room was to house a whole family of five to six people.

Now, a month after Pearl Harbor, emptying our homes occupied all our time. My sister still went to classes at high school, and my younger brother, in elementary, went under protest. There was much to dispose of, all our furniture and clothes, our books, mementos of our family. Not much we owned was of fine quality, but the Salvation Army gladly accepted everything. They had owned a barn-like building for years on the outskirts of Japantown that housed homeless Japanese orphans and families. After the evacuation, people from Oklahoma, refugees from the dust bowl, would be housed there, we were told.

Of course there were vulture-like people who offered a pittance for goods my folks wanted to sell. Well, we were well into the Great Depression, and everyone was hurting. Mom and Pop sold or gave away everything until the house was nearly empty. Our beds, chairs and tables were to go to the Salvation Army after we left. We pared our belongings down to whatever would fit into two suitcases per family member. That was one of the rulings that came with the WCCA plan for our evacuation, and we thought we might as well get used to living sparsely. For meals we used up all the rice from the hundred pound sacks that Mom always had on hand, plus all the pickles she had made and canned. We bought fish and meat that were available from the nearby Chinese restaurant owner who sympathized with us, as the Japanese grocery shops were now closed.

With the group of men working in the WCCA, Tommy and I were told to go to San Bruno, a little town south of San Francisco. There we were to prepare to house the evacuees from the entire Bay Area. The place even had a name, The Tanforan Assembly Center. There were to be 80,000 citizens incarcerated there, and let me not neglect to say that Tanforan was a former racetrack that housed hundreds of horses. It sickened me when I learned that thousands of human beings were going to be living in those horse stalls.

Chapter 9

April 28, 1942

The day I left home was the blackest day of my life. Tommy and I were taken in an unmarked government sedan from the corner of Buchanan and Post streets to a downtown building, then in a Greyhound bus to the Tanforan Racetrack in San Bruno. It would be a few days before most of my Japanese neighbors were going to experience this humiliating expulsion. I was part of the team of Nisei (second generation Americans), who would keep order among the citizens arriving there next week, and assign them their living quarters.

When Tommy and I first went to the WCCA's (Wartime Civilian Control Agency) offices downtown to apply for the job, we had not been greeted warmly, to put it mildly. The agency workers reluctantly signed up about a dozen Japanese Americans, and if the choices had been up to them, we—who looked like the enemy and strangers to their social circles— would never have been hired. They patronizingly gave us bits of information, such as how barbed wire fence surrounded the entire racetrack, how the watchtowers had guards with machine guns, and how searchlight beams scanned the place at night. We were told about the "feeding" hours and the government's plans to build more barracks for additional mess halls. They questioned us with suspicion about our Japanese language skills, and told us to nip in the bud any mob violence. I could sense that they were afraid such attacks were going to happen to them. On top of that, they told us that we were going to be leaving our homes in a few days. Tommy and I felt glum about the whole meeting when we left.

Until that time our family life had its steady routine: work, school, study, regular chores and quiet social activities in the confines of the lifestyle of a typical hard-working yet poor family of the Depression.

Carrying on bravely while in shock after Pearl Harbor, my mother broke down when she heard that I was going to this camp prior to the family. This separation, if only for a few days, had her on edge so badly that Papa and I had to assure her that I would be safe with Tommy and a few college friends, and that we were all going to be working together. She finally did put on a calm exterior for my sake, as well as to keep my younger brother and sister from starting to imagine terrible things about my sudden disappearance from their lives.

So, there I was, standing on the corner in Japantown, San Francisco, gazing around for the last time at the only home that I'd ever known—a place that held my first and deeply cherished memories. It was just before sunrise, with no one about on a quiet street with faded gray-blue houses and storefronts that were beginning to lighten up as the sun silently began shining on them. Also standing with me, sadness etched on their faces, were my parents and siblings. A few feet away was Tommy's family, also feeling the same sense of doom, all of us wondering how we were going to survive the war, or if we would see San Francisco ever again.

As soon as we saw the sedan slowing down to pick us up, Tommy and I gathered our suitcases, and simply nodded good-bye to our families, and got in the car. We were brought up not to gush, kiss, or embrace each other in public. In fact, we did not display such emotions at home either. The last thing I saw from the window of the car through misty eyes was our families waving slowly with peculiarly wan smiles.

We later got transferred to a Greyhound bus at another location downtown, from where we rode with the Caucasian staff and the other Nisei workers. Our two suitcases were filled with sweaters, shirts, underwear, jackets, slacks and shoes. Tommy fitted in a pack of cards, and I had squeezed in my Monopoly set, crossword magazines, plenty of paper, and pens and pencils.

The bus ride took a couple of hours, and it was comforting to have Tommy sitting next to me as we headed to this former racetrack in a little town called San Bruno, just south of the City. We were silent and our eyes drank in everything on the road leading away from our homes. We wanted to imprint this ride in our minds as a never-to-be-forgotten turning point in our lives. My stomach churned with the bile coming up, and I fought hard not to embarrass myself by making a mess and stinking up this bus.

Truth to tell, my first sight of the Tanforan Racetrack was of a huge and attractive, well-landscaped park. Well, no wonder. It was built for the pleasure and comfort of people seeking amusement at a sports stadium. The irony of it made me sneer. Our families had never had the means of spending time in a place such as this, what with our noses always to the grindstone, but now it was going to be forced upon us.

Once off the bus, we had a brief meeting at the grandstand, where we were given a map of the racetrack, then told to become familiar with its layout. Imagine my dismay when, after walking around the existing buildings and newly built barracks, we came to the horse stalls where some families were going to be housed—row upon row of paint-worn buildings, sending off whiffs of horseshit. What had my people done to deserve this? *This is America,* I thought, *not Nazi Germany. American citizens were going to live in THAT?* Tommy and I looked at each other. Our families with five or six people could not fit in horse stalls— or rather, the cots could not. Smaller families of two to four would have to though, poor souls. I looked in several stalls, all reeking of horse droppings, and saw that they had only been given a cursory wash down.

Tommy angrily and loudly pointed out these filthy stalls to the office crew. They told him dismissively that the new residents could wash and sweep them down if they so desired. Across the way there was one fairly clean line of stalls near a watchtower. It was so clean, I made note of it, as well as the little park-like area next to it, where a small group of residents could sit under the trees to read or chat quietly. *Variations in hell.*

Our Nisei group, a dozen of us bilingual college men, were then given more detailed maps so we'd learn the location of all public buildings, the mess halls, the administration offices, the laundry and latrine buildings.

Back inside the grandstand, we were taken through its various levels and shown where the business offices were. The entire upper floor was like an open barn. It had been converted into a dormitory for single men. Bunk beds—there must have been close to five hundred of them—were neatly lined up and taking up the entire floor space. Our duties were to placate and keep order among the disgruntled residents. Tommy was a social creature and I knew he would be sought for comfort and aid, but I was not quite as gregarious, and felt inadequate for the job.

"Now," said the director, "we will assign your living quarters. Those of you from small families of three or four, go to that line to the left and select a horse stall. Those from larger families, line up on the right and select a room in the barracks section. I suggest that you choose one close to these offices so we can reach you quickly. In a few days the first arrivals will be here, hundreds of them. There is only one entrance to this compound, so you can expect a lot of chaos. All of you will be there to check names and the number of people in each family, and then send them to their respective units. Keep everyone moving. We've already found other young men to take charge of the suitcases and larger cartons that people will be bringing in. We know there's going to be confusion and short tempers, so I leave it up to you to keep the crowd in order. The mess hall should be open shortly before their arrival. We get food supplies from the Army, so expect the usual pork and beans and Spam. By the way, we in the office staff will be eating the same things."

Tommy and I each chose a barrack room close to the offices for our families. When we checked the rooms out we were relieved that they were clean, with cots, mattresses, sheets, blankets and pillows, all that GI stuff stacked in a corner. Heck, five people sleeping in a 20x26 room sure didn't leave much space for anything. We put two cots together for our parents, and two close together for my brother and me. We gave my sister her own space. I guess I should have been glad we had such accommodations with the cots. Imagine the poor families who were going to be living in the horse stalls, breathing in the animal stink and trying to sleep on hay mattresses.

Privacy was a laughable thought. We took for granted that rooms always had doors. Then, I berated myself, *Privacy? Forget privacy. What do you want? The damn government is sheltering us and feeding us—more likely acting like it has a guilty conscience.*

Chapter 10

(Marissa, I wanted you to know what is was like that first day in Tanforan for your mother when I met her. . I inserted this chapter here to tie it in with my own story.)

Tanforan, California
May 1, 1942

The middle-aged couple, Ken and Chiyoko Araki sat on an army cot, speechless, with heads bowed. They were in a horse stall, having just arrived from their San Francisco home. This was to be their living quarters until further notice.

As soon as he could speak, Ken said in a low voice, "A fine thing, eh? We're worse off than animals. Three and four people in a stall that used to hold only one horse."

"Uh-huh. Terrible", said his wife, nodding with a neutral expression. They faced the painted white wall six feet across from them. The distance from the front door with a tiny window beside it, was eight feet to the back to a Dutch door from where the stall extended eight feet into a dark windowless back "room."

Outside, their seventeen-year-old daughter, Tomiko, was shaking out army blankets, grateful to be doing this vigorous task while letting off steam. Across the way, she saw men sweeping out their stalls, spewing out foul-sounding words in acrid tones she'd never heard before. *They're really bitter, just like they're ready to kill someone.*

Her mother, Chiyo, stuck her head out and said, "Better come in, Tomi-chan. You don't have to listen to those people. We all feel the same—humiliated beyond words and helpless to do anything about it, but we're not going to let this get us down."

Until a few months before Tomiko had been a typical high school student, carefree with high hopes and plans for her graduation party, in a new evening gown for the dance, then entering the University of California at Berkeley. Her world turned upside down when Pearl Harbor was bombed, and America was plunged into war, into World War II.

The morning's bus trip to this blasted racetrack was the final straw. All the Japanese residents in San Francisco had known only a week before that they were going to be sent here, and were now living out of their allotted two suitcases. "Only what you can carry," they were told. In the meantime the thought of being forced to leave the only home she had ever known created a violent reaction within her. *No wonder people go into a rage, lash out, and shoot each other*, she reflected.

"Don't take this personally, Tomi-chan," her mother said to her. "We're only a part of a war plan, and individuals' feelings are of no importance." She knew how very sensitive a teenager could be, even under normal circumstances.

"Yes, I know that, but it's so unfair. We're *American* citizens! They've officially classified us as enemy aliens and we're forced out of our homes and put into these horseshit stalls! For crying out loud, how much more salt are they going to pour into our wounds?"

"What's that saying, 'All's fair in love and war'? Here's a good example of it. People in the past have experienced unfairness, and this saying applies to us now."

Mama's pretty wise. Good defense mechanism. That's probably why she and Papa can seem unruffled as they carry on.

Papa was busy setting up the cots, brushing off the mattresses, and installing the lock holder at the doorway.

"Mama," Tomiko said, looking at her new wrist watch that her parents had bought ahead of time for her graduation present, "It's almost lunchtime now. We're in Group 1, so we'll be eating right at noon."

"Come, Papa," her mother said, "We might as well close up and walk over to the grandstand. What do they call it, a 'mess hall'? Let's hope we'll meet some of our former neighbors and friends along the way."

Papa was not hungry; he wanted to set out a few things from his suitcase, and just putter around. His stomach was in a knot, and he needed to assuage his anger and hatred against an invisible bunch of people powerful enough to cause this nightmare he was now plunged in. Living in a horse stall, for god's sake! Struggling to snap himself into a more decent mood, he said as pleasantly as possible, "Oh, alright, I really wanted to settle in more, but we have all the time in the world from now on, don't we? I'm glad I was at least able to sweep out this place and set up our cots. Well, here are the keys to our new home, ladies."

Mama brought out two pairs of chopsticks from her suitcase because she heard that everyone would be issued army type dishes and cups, but certainly no chopsticks. "We were told that after we eat, we should wash our dishes in the laundry room. Let's look for one on the way to the grandstand. Oh, yes, we need to know where the latrines are, too."

"There's the laundry room and the latrines are right next door," said Tomiko pointing to the right. "One thing about our place, it's fairly close to everything. I took a little walk before I shook out the blankets, and noticed that it's quiet here because we're at the edge of the campground. The train runs by only a few feet behind our stalls every day, a man told me. I also noticed a tiny park right by it and was surprised how nice it felt.

"Yes, I saw that place", said Mama. "It's grassy with trees lining the fence, and is inviting. Anything that pleasant is so welcome. The only bad thing is the watchtower right over those trees, though." No use mentioning the machine guns mounted by the window aimed at the camp, or the occasional movement of the lone soldier up there, and that barbed wire fence, reminding them they were prisoners. Chiyo knew that it was useless to say too much, with her family preoccupied in their misery and black thoughts.

As they approached the grandstand toward the center of the racetrack, they saw other families also heading that way. They bowed to each other. One woman asked, "Where are you folks from? We're from Oakland."

"We're from San Francisco," Mama replied. "Did you get much notice about coming here?"

"Yes, in Oakland and Berkeley, we were notified almost a month ago, and the waiting was trying for us. At the last minute, they made us get our smallpox vaccines, and we all got pretty sick. Good thing we didn't have to go to work or send the kids to school."

"We had our shots a month ago. You're right. Lucky we didn't have to go to work either. My daughter was finished with school and she didn't get too sick from the vaccination, but my husband and I got high fever. It must be terrible to get the real thing, like in the old days when there was no cure for smallpox."

They met others as they continued walking, and Mama and Papa were delighted to see a few neighbors from back home. Tomiko barely knew them so she kept going, hoping to meet someone she knew from school.

There was a long line outside the grandstand, from where they could smell pork and beans. After the early morning breakfast before their departure from home, Tomiko realized how hungry she was. *So, this is what the*

British mean by a "queue." They've been at war for a long time now, and I heard that they had to line up for everything. Well, now, we're in the same boat.

Once inside, they first came to a long table piled high with trays. The next table held stacks of blue and white enamel plates, bowls, and coffee mugs. They took one of each. The next table had trays filled with forks, knives, and spoons, which they also took. At last, they reached the cafeteria-style steam table holding three pans filled with pork and beans. They were hungry enough that it smelled so good, but the actual sight of the food took away much of their appetites.

"Better take a spoonful," said Papa. "Just to fill ourselves."

A few people's plates were filled with the beans, only because they liked them. Everyone else passed on them.

Tomiko was hungry enough, so she took a slice of white bread and spooned out a generous amount of pork and beans over it. "I'm going to close my eyes and imagine that I'm eating a good beef stew."

"You might as well," encouraged Papa, relieved that his daughter was making the best of it.

They came to one big pan with slices of meat. "What is that?" asked Mama when the cook walked by.

"This is Spam, Oba-san. *Mazui yo.*" (Tastes lousy, missus), he said sympathetically.

"Oh, if we put shoyu on it, it'll become edible," said Mama.

"Oba-san, *lady*, they don't even know what shoyu is at the commissary, otherwise we would have ordered gallons of it."

Women in line behind her laughed. "Sato-joyu (sugar and shoyu) works like magic on the worst tasting food!", she shouted, at which everyone agreed loudly.

"Bah, these women," grumbled one man standing

impatiently behind them. "They think they're here on vacation cackling away, while our sons are pulled into the army and getting killed."

The man behind him grunted in agreement.

After helping themselves to salad, then Jell-O for dessert, they looked around for white rice, their daily staple, but found none. One woman asked the cook if there would be any. He shrugged and said, "They didn't send any over, just the white bread. You get what the soldiers get, missus."

So with plates of food minus white rice, everyone sat down to their first meal at the racetrack.

"Funny, we didn't see any of our friends there at lunch," said Mama.

"They must still be back in San Francisco, or else they're living in the barracks and they're on a different shift," said Papa. "I've already seen people from Berkeley I've heard about. At least, I can try to make new acquaintances here. They'd be easy to talk to, not like some of the ones from the farm country."

Tomiko went to the laundry room where she rinsed off all the dishes in the laundry tub. She bowed to the old ladies who were doing the same at the next tub.

"I hear we'll have hot water for our laundry very soon," said one lady, "And these tubs have to be filled two inches with cold water before adding the hot water, otherwise, the poor quality of this cement causes them to crack."

"Oh, imagine that," said Tomiko. She couldn't care less, but politely made small talk with her. *Boy, I can see how exciting life is going to be here.*

On the way back to her horse stall a tall fellow came up to her, smiling.

"Hi, how're you doing?"

"So far, so good, at least we have a roof over our heads and we even got fed a full meal." *Who is he?* Tomiko wondered.

As if reading her thoughts, he said, "Guess you don't remember me from when all you folks got off the bus and I assigned your living quarters."

"Oh, of course," she said. "It was all so new and scary, but it comes back to me now. I do remember how you were looking over the list and shuffling through the big address cards until you found the right one for us." She gave him a big smile.

"Pretty observant, aren't you?"

"First impressions, I'd say."

God, she's pretty, and so nice to talk to. Wonder who she is, and why I never saw her before in San Francisco.

"Were you at Cal? What's your name? I'm George Ohara."

"I'm Tomiko Araki, but no, I wasn't at Cal. I just graduated from Lowell High School."

Oh, god, women like to look younger than they actually are. Wonder if that made her mad. "Well, I never saw you before in San Francisco. I'm from Japantown myself."

"We lived on Webster near Clay Street, a short distance from Japantown, although Mama went there to buy Japanese food."

George was pleased with himself and went on, "I went to Lowell, too, but I graduated four years ago, then went straight to Cal."

"Oh, yes, I was ready to apply to Cal, but you know … What did you major in?"

"Biology, and ready to start my senior year," said George. Then his face fell, "Like you say,' but you know' . . ."

"Hey, George, they want you in the office in ten minutes

for some meeting!" shouted a fellow from down the road.

"That's my buddy, Tommy Miyamoto. We've been pals since we were kids. Well, I'll be seeing you around, Tomiko."

"Nice talking to you, George. I hope to see you again, too."

She hopes to see me again. Hot diggity! With a smile on his face, George hurried off toward Tommy.

"What the heck are you smiling about, unless it's that girl you were talking to?" teased Tommy.

George was blushing, stammering, "Nah, I remember giving her family one of the better stalls on block five, and she remembered me."

"She must be something special ... Gawd, George, wipe that goofy look off your face."

Chapter 11

The way of life for thousands of incarcerated people at a racetrack near San Francisco presented an unusual sight—that is, if anyone had been there to observe the scene. In the middle of the week entire families dressed in faded, worn clothing walked leisurely about in the sunshine, on and off the grassy fairway. It was a June day in 1942, an hour after lunchtime—a time when most people would be at work and their kids at school, but every one of these men, women and children were confined here. And it was only because they looked like Jap enemies, not like the good American citizens they were.

Where, except in the Orient, would one see a crowd of people milling about in one location, most of them with jet-black hair? Standing around the open window of a small adobe building, a handful of people were listening intently to a pianist playing Chopin's *Fantaisie-Impromptu* ... "How beautiful that sounds," they whispered, nodding sadly to each other. Their faces revealed how much they wanted to go in to watch the pianist, but they knew they would disturb him. "He just returned from a concert tour in Europe," someone quietly remarked with sadness. Clucking their tongues, they sighed, "What a shame."

When the pianist came to an especially lyrical passage, one gray-haired lady murmured, "Ahhhh, to think that beauty such as this can be found in an unexpected moment and place, even when living in a horse stall, while people are killing each other all around the world and destroying their cities."

Others nodded in agreement, then one by one they began to disperse, some unable to lift the gloom shrouding their spirits while others feigned cheerfulness as they took their children's hands. They walked away in all directions, some toward the dusty dirt road leading to the horse stalls that had become their living quarters. Two older men in shabby clothes still stayed, smirking and asking each other what was so good about a Japanese man playing the piano, "for Christ sake, a white woman's la-di-da past time."

Six months had passed since Pearl Harbor. Everyone at the racetrack had been forced out of their home and faced future uncertainties. Of course, they were not the only ones for whom life had turned into a nightmare. All over America shocked citizens were living under fear and doubt.

The people in Tanforan were there under Executive Order 9066 issued by Franklin Delano Roosevelt decreeing that, **"All persons of Japanese ancestry will be removed from their homes on the West Coast for the duration of the War."** It did not matter that they were American citizens. After debates in Congress the Department of Defense was put in charge, and it declared the entire West Coast to be a military zone. There was no due process of law, and there were no trials; there was simply a decree that the **"Presence of possible spies for Japan among the Japanese population made it mandatory that all Japanese be removed from the West Coast."**

Before becoming imprisoned in this former racetrack Japanese men in the San Francisco Bay Area were forced to hurriedly close the businesses that they had patiently built up over the years, and worked hard to keep going through the Depression. They operated in a daze, numbly watching their life's work come crashing down with each item being carted from their stores, dental or medical offices. A few were fortunate to sell to local buyers, but since many of them ran shops that catered to Japanese family needs they grimly took their losses and shuttered their business places within three or four months after Pearl Harbor. Added to the bitterness of tearing down their work when business had started to improve after the Depression was the shock that was more than these men could bear.

This deplorable situation was repeated throughout the West Coast, including every single major city from San Diego, Los Angeles, Sacramento, Portland and Seattle. This mass move affected 120,000 Japanese people, one third of them immigrants, and the rest American citizens.

George's mother recalled the hectic weeks of clearing their home before the imposed deadline. Getting rid of papers and documents was an endless, time-consuming chore. She was in and out of her backyard, dumping papers and photographs in piles to burn each night: school papers, report cards and newspaper clippings of events that were important at the time—each piece of paper overwhelming her with sad memories of happier years.

Lost in thought, she had been startled when her neighbor called over the back fence, "*Kon-nichi wa, Ohara-san.*" (Good Day to you, Mrs. Ohara.) Since the fence was only four feet high, they could see each other. "*Ahhh, Yanagi-san, ikaga desu ka?*" (Oh, Mrs. Yanagi, how are you?)

"Every day, I resolve to get rid of huge piles of junk, but after living here for over twenty years, I get distracted and find things I'd completely forgotten about."

Nodding vigorously, Mrs. Ohara laughed and shouted in agreement, "Yes! I'm having the same problem. Some days, all I get done is to look at the things that I know should go into the trash, and at the end of the day, find that they are still sitting around the house."

"Not only that, we have so much furniture, you know," said Mrs. Yanagi. "My husband and I want to sell the dining set we finally bought after saving money for it for over a year."

"Oh, yes, I remember it was last year when you had a big New Year's feast at your house, and a dozen people were squeezed around that beautiful table." Mrs. Ohara smiled broadly, adding, "It was indeed a wonderful party."

Mrs. Yanagi started to say something but could no longer control herself, and covered her face as tears streamed down her cheeks. "Oh, we were always so grateful to live this well in America after the hard life in Japan; but now, all I feel is misery and despair that is deeper than what I ever knew in Japan."

"*Tada-ima!*" (We're home!), shouted two children from the front door as it banged shut.

"Oh, Yanagi-san, the children are home from school, so please excuse me," Mrs. Ohara said gently and with a look of sympathy. She was glad for the boisterous interruption, bowed to Mrs. Yanagi, and hurried inside to greet the children, relieved that she was spared more gloom from further conversation.

That night, when her husband came home for his twice-weekly nights off, Mrs. Ohara asked if he had heard any official directives about their situation. "Not really," Mr. Ohara said somberly. "Just that Japanese submarines were sighted off the coast so the government is anxious to get us out of here. Make sure the kids come straight home from school, and no playing outside like they used to."

Mrs. Ohara was frightened and added to her husband's warnings, "I heard at the store that the Japanese Army is in Alaska, and they plan to make their way down through Canada and all the way down the West Coast."

"Yes, I know. . . I wasn't going to tell you anything like that and scare you, Mama, but be ready to pull the kids out of school if necessary. I've been following news articles about how the English are coping with Nazi bombings in London and their larger cities, and the main thing is that they try to follow as normal a routine as they can each day. Sadly, their children have been sent off to live with strangers in the country. What that must do to little kids."

Mrs. Ohara nodded sympathetically, sighing, "Poor, innocent victims."

Mr. Ohara hesitated before adding, "The FBI makes surprise visits here in *Nohonjin-machi*, Japantown, and have taken away many of our neighborhood leaders. Since I never got involved with community activities, they may not come around looking for me. After all, I practically live where I work."

Mrs. Ohara did not tell her husband that ever since she had heard about these men being hauled away suddenly, she spent each day worried sick that he too would be taken in for questioning. So far, those men had not been heard from, and their families were frantic not to be told where they were. At least her husband, being a butler at a businessman's home, had little occasion to participate in Japantown's social and community events over the years and was not a familiar figure in the neighborhood.

After a moment of gathering his thoughts, Mr. Ohara continued, "As for us being uprooted and sent away, I understand from what George tells me, this new government agency that he works for has a two-step plan for evacuation. First, they've taken over places like fairgrounds or former CCC camps with facilities that will each hold several thousand people. After we have all been evacuated from our homes and into these camps, the second step is to transfer us to places in remote inland states and imprison us there for the duration of the war."

Mrs. Ohara was listening closely. "You mean they're going to move us around two and three times? Can you imagine what this will be like for families with small children, or for the real old people?"

"Ironical, isn't it?" said Mr. Ohara. "Our fondest dreams when we first married were to travel if we ever became rich. Do you remember?"

"Ahh yes, those sweet dreams when we were young," sighed his wife.

As it turned out, Tanforan racetrack became the first center to confine the thousands of Japanese people who had been living in the San Francisco Bay area.

For a time Tanforan had been the home of the famous racehorse Seabiscuit. It was a well-established site with pleasant landscaping in the public areas around the grandstand with many small buildings scattered throughout the park. The racetrack had been vacant for some years and was considered to be a suitable temporary holding area that could easily accommodate a population of seven thousand people. Small families of two to four members were to be housed in the horse stalls, while larger families of five or six members were cramped into rooms in barracks that were hurriedly being built. To stave off idleness and mischief, makeshift classrooms for children were to be held in the mess halls, so they would be under supervision part of each day. School supplies were nonexistent, and the teachers and their assistants winged each day's activities doing craftwork, storytelling, sing-alongs, outdoor sports, and games. Once a week old movies were shown at night in the grandstand for everyone. Most people went at first, even the old folks who hardly spoke English, staring at the Tom Mix or Hopalong Cassidy westerns.

After a month of observing how camp life was progressing, the administration and the Nisei assistants noted the necessity to assign neighborhood chores to maintain sanitary conditions for such a large population. Committees were formed. In rotation involving as many volunteers as were available, one team cleaned the latrine and laundry rooms, with a plumber who was always available and called upon often; another group cleaned the mess halls; certain people kept pathways swept (twice a day if necessary); and still others would do the evening rounds to ensure that roll call was taken and the curfew observed. It was hoped that eventually a few natural leaders would emerge to represent the residents' complaints or requests to the administration. Since Tanforan was within the city limits of San Bruno, the city's fire department helped establish and train a volunteer crew of firefighters within the camp in the event they were ever needed.

Chapter 12

It was at the Tanforan Assembly Center that George and Tomiko found themselves, he having spotted her as an unusually winsome girl when she arrived at the camp. He was taken with the sudden appearance of her dimples when she smiled at him, along with her sweet voice. Her family was among the first in his line, and he assigned them a horse stall in what he considered the best location. In their free time (which was almost always), George and Tomiko became part of a group of young people who gathered everyday after lunch at a little park at the edge of the campground. It was a pleasant, grassy spot that they found inviting, even though it was against the barbed wire fence. They would stand together under tall eucalyptus trees longingly watching cars and trucks speeding by on the Bayshore Highway as they aired the helplessness and bitterness they felt as American citizens impounded in their own country as "non-aliens", a term as scornful as "enemy aliens". They found solace in each other's company; it mattered not that they were sitting right under one of the camp's watchtowers. At first they were wary of the lone soldier up there with a machine gun pointed at the campground, but never having experienced violence, these young city people, even though uneasy, doubted that these guns would ever be used.

One day, during the change of guards, a soldier from the tower slowly climbed down the ladder to go off-duty. Watching the group of young people on the other side of the barbed wire fence, he nodded to them. Like them, he was in his late teens. When he reached the ground, he suddenly stopped short, startled that he recognized a couple of them. "Hey, girls, don't I know you?" he shouted, pointing to two girls. "Oh yeah … from Lowell High? You used to play the piano, didn't you?" he said, gesturing at Tomiko.

The young people cautiously approached the fence, coming face-to-face with the guard and staring at this stranger who claimed to know them.

The two girls studied him more closely. Suddenly Tomiko gasped, "Is that really you, uh … John McMillan? Oh, my goodness, what are you doing here? Are you really a guard here?"

"Yeah, you got it. I volunteered right after Pearl Harbor and got sent here after basic training. I thought I recognized you the other day from up there," he said pointing to the watchtower. "Boy oh boy, I'm telling you, war stinks."

After a moment's silence, Tomiko's friend Gracie shouted, "Ohh, I know you! You were in the band and the ROTC. I used to see you in your uniform, marching around the school yard during drills and giving orders." Her enthusiasm was catching, and typical of young people, they all began smiling.

"Yup. I sure liked being a leader in the ROTC band, but now I realize how different it is to actually be in the Army. Believe me, everyone, it can get ugly … bah!" he spat out. "We were taught how to kill people. At school, it was like play," he continued, but wanting to lighten the mood he waved his hand toward Tomiko. "Speaking of school days, you played the piano real good at the dance in the gym that day."

Tomiko sputtered, then blushed, "Wha--? Oh, my goodness … that fire drill!"

"It was a last-minute dance right after a fire drill towards the end of the day," Gracie added excitedly as she also recalled that incident, and nudged Tomiko.

"Oh, yeah," said McMillan. "That silly fire drill saved my life though. It got me out of my trig class." Slowly, as more of that incident came back to him, he smiled. "Good thing the teachers decided it was the best way to keep all of us orderly. Yeah, we danced and danced to your music until the final bell. Gee, that was just swell. I'll never forget that day, like I said, because I was sweating over not turning in my homework." Then his eyes snapped to the present and he said sadly, "You know, those were the good old days, it turns out. Who would'a dreamt that we'd come to anything this horrible?" A somber air passed on both sides of the barbed wire fence as everyone was hit once again with the reality of the wretched conditions that had befallen them since Pearl Harbor.

George, too, was taking all this in. *Tomiko plays piano, huh? No wonder she hums a lot, she must be singing inside herself all the time. And her steps are so lively when we go on our walks—I love the way her ponytail swishes and her thick black hair shines in the sunlight.*

"Hey, kids, I gotta go," shouted McMillan. "I'm off the next four hours, then have ta report back at 7:30. If you can make it, come back and see if I'm on duty here. Sometimes they have me marching around the front of this place, it depends ... So long, see ya."

The young people waved back, their spirits buoyed by this turn of events, having talked to someone on the outside.

"Imagine! A classmate from school," said Tomiko. "Let's come by after dinner and see if he's on duty. They're showing a movie tonight, but it's always cowboy stuff or something second-rate, so we won't miss anything good."

"But even going to those movies was better than doing nothing, at first," piped up Yukio.   George had his own thought. *If that soldier isn't in the tower tonight, I've got a better plan.*

As it turned out, the soldier was not at the tower after dinner, so George led them to a small, darkened building. "C'mon, I've got a better idea for some fun." He opened the door to the building where the pianist practiced every day. "Good, it's unlocked, so we're in luck," he said as he stepped inside and flipped the light switch.

'Hey, what is this?" everyone asked in unison, craning their necks and tiptoeing into a spacious room that was barely furnished except for two chairs and a table along the wall—and a grand piano. Cobwebs hung in the corners and around the windows, and everything inside was dusty. There was a lot of open space in the center of the room. Tomiko opened the piano and ran her fingers over the keys. "Wow! A Mason and Hamlin! Not bad for horse-stall residents," she said, continuing to play arpeggios up and down the keyboard, impressing her new friends. "And it's in tune!"

"Yeah, I did that," said Eddie. "I heard that pianist practicing and noticed how this thing was so badly out of tune, so I told them at the office I'd volunteer to tune the piano. You see, I used to be the choir director at our church, so I told them at the office that I'm hoping to start a choral group here and get people to join it as a group activity. And they told me to go ahead."

"What? How the heck did you get them to agree to that?" asked George. "Didn't think the office would be concerned about an out-of-tune piano or a church choir."

"Heck, they don't know what they're doing in the office yet," Tommy piped in. "Their main concern is to keep the camp running smoothly, and that everyone behaves. The thought of mob violence scares them out of their wits. I know that the staff is suspicious of all of us, and the only reason we were hired is that they need us for crowd control and because we can talk to the old people in Japanese so they can understand what needs to be done."

"Things are slowly getting organized though," added Eddie. "Look, they've got the San Bruno Fire Department coming over each week to train our volunteer crew; the cooks in the mess halls are pretty set with their duties and schedules; and they are going to assign block managers to take care of housing problems. The infirmary is also running well, with the few Nisei doctors and nurses taking care of sick people, and more medical equipment and supplies are being brought in. We'll have the same medical equipment they have at regular Army bases. The main office gets orders and memos from the big shots in the WCCA, and everyone in the office, including us, is putting in their two cents. It'll all settle down in a few more weeks, I think."

The girls couldn't have been less interested and started to chatter about old women using washboards to scrub their families' clothes and sheets by hand in the laundry room right next to the latrines. They giggled about seeing a lot of panties and half-slips made of old flour sacks. And they were warned about some old men who pretended not to know the difference between the men's and women's latrines and walked into the women's latrines all the time. The girls also thought it awful that there were no doors or curtains for the toilets or the showers stalls, and how their mothers insisted that a girl never go into those buildings alone.

"C'mon, Tomiko, why don't you start playing, " said Eddie, suddenly impatient. He turned to the others, saying, "Let's sing along with her, and if anyone wants to dance, we can do that too."

Tomiko was overjoyed to be with people her age. She hadn't played since selling her piano after the war started. She delighted in the beautiful tones of the piano as it tinkled the beginning of "Three Little Fishes," which had everyone singing and rolling their eyes, their moods lifting with each verse. They liked that so much, she followed with "Night and Day," a tune that inspired several guys to take girls' hands and lead them to the center of the room to dance. Others followed, and before long, the whole crowd was squeezed closely together and dancing to "I'm Getting Sentimental Over You." No one wanted to stop so Tomiko played another tune, "I'll Walk Alone."

When she saw George holding a different girl closely with each tune, she wanted to dance herself, especially as she played her favorite, "I'll Never Smile Again." With no one else to play the piano, Tomiko decided she'd end with "Deep Purple," and then closed the keyboard as a hint that she was quitting.

"Oh, don't quit, Tomi!" implored the girls. "Just one more. Please, pretty please? How about "Dream"?

"Oh, yes, Tomi!" pleaded the fellows, so Tomiko gave in and started playing, but deliberately looked down so she wouldn't catch George holding another girl close to him, too close for her to care to see.

When she finished playing she could see that the music had put everyone in too romantic a mood, so she banged out "Don't Sit Under The Apple Tree," for a change of pace. She was glad that this tune forced them out of that dreamy trance in each other's arms into a jumpy, playful mood.

While the dancers were catching their breath after that, applause came from the doorway. "Young lady, that was a treat," said a tall, older fellow who stood there clapping. He had walked by the building during the middle of the dancing and stood listening and watching. He approached Tomiko as George rushed to join them.

"Hi, we were just passing the time. I'm George Ohara." He nodded.

"And I'm Kim Shimada from Berkeley."

George tried to be friendly with this new fellow and continued, "We usually get together at the park under the watchtower, but one of the guards wasn't there tonight. We were just about to go there now to see if he's back on duty. He talked to us this afternoon, and it turns out he went to school with several of the girls."

Kim stiffened with shock. "*What?* You talked to the guard, an American soldier?" he sounded frantic. "How come? He could shoot you. Crazy things happen, you know. Better be careful—everyone's on edge." He was incredulous that these young kids dared to talk to a white man outside the barbed wire fence, an American soldier at that. He couldn't believe how they were so naive and trusting, like babies. Calming down slightly, he said more quietly, "Anyway, I needed to get out of our place. I've been sulking around far too long in our barrack room, where things aren't good. My father had a stroke right after Pearl Harbor and is having trouble getting around; and boy, is he depressed. My poor Mom's in a fog, and my younger brother and sisters are no big help. You know how it is ... When I saw all of you having a good time, and heard all that good music, I had to come in." He turned to George and asked him in a low voice, "That piano player, she's nice. Is she a girlfriend?"

"Naw, I just met her, but we hit it off pretty good, that's all."

"You know," said Kim frowning, "at a time like this, it's hard to think beyond the moment. I had a nice girlfriend named Eileen at Berkeley, but they sent her family to a camp called Manzanar because their home was in San Jose. I was going to ask her to marry me eventually. It's almost like the way the old slaves' families were broken up when being sold according to owners' needs."

George nodded. *Cripes, what a comparison. Holy moly, man, this guy sure is bitter.*

Kim continued, "You and I might get called up and be in some special army unit, segregated like they're doing with the Hawaiian Nisei soldiers, and then we'll just become cannon fodder. None of that dumb self-sacrifice idealism for me. No sir. Never! I'm hoping that since I'm bilingual—and with rumors that the army is thinking of using interpreters over in the South Pacific—I can question the Japanese soldiers who are captured over there. That way, I will be doing my duty."

George welcomed conversation with this man who talked about things he hadn't stopped to think through. He'd been around too many people in Japantown who were emotional to the point of hysteria, unable to think clearly anymore.

"Hey, if you're from Berkeley, did you go to Cal, Kim?"

"Yeah, I just graduated ... to this lofty way of life," he spat, as he waved his hand around the room, eyes shooting out rays of anger.

"I don't know which is worse," George replied, shrugging, "having one more year to go like me, or already having a degree like you. Can't you go back East and continue, or get a teaching position? They're not so prejudiced about us in that part of the country. Uh, just stay away from the South, though. They call us "high yaller" down there."

Kim paused, shaking his head in frustration. "I've thought of all that. I could have gone right after the war started, but they restricted us from traveling shortly afterwards. But more importantly, I'm the oldest son and must stay with my family. Good thing I stuck around, with Pop getting sick. I had to do all the closing up of our house and help Mom care for him. Even though my teenage siblings helped (with much prodding), they were so confused, and not that useful. My Pop is a strong pro-Japan man, having worked among rednecks who made him feel unwelcome in this country. It's sad because Pop, like so many others, came to America with big dreams and high hopes, only to get beaten down through the years. Yeah, it's been pretty rough."

Kim was surprised to find himself telling a stranger this much, like he needed to be confessing all his thoughts to a sympathetic ear. He was always more reserved, especially with someone he had just met. *What's come over me? I guess I really needed to air out my furor. Boy, I was going on nonstop there, but I feel better now.*

After trying to decide whether or not to say any more, he whispered to George, "Hey, let's close up here and let the others go ahead and check out your soldier friend up in the tower. I, uh, want to tell you something I heard." *There I go, blabbing away again, but then, this kid seems to understand me and he sure has a way of making me want to talk.*

"Yeah?" said George, his curiosity piqued by Kim's wariness.

The two walked slowly, hanging back from the rest of the group that had left the music room. "I heard rumors," Kim said in a hushed voice, "That Mike. . ."

"Good evening, gentlemen," came a sharp-sounding voice behind them.

George and Kim whirled around to see the block captain approaching them.

"You know that in a little while, it's going to be roll call."

They both kept walking, and Kim, especially annoyed by the man's officious attitude, made a sweeping motion with his left arm to check his wristwatch. "Oh yes, but we still have a whole half hour. We'll be home by nine o'clock. Thank you, sir."

"Give guys like him a chore, and they begin to strut around like they're in charge of running this whole camp," mumbled George as they rounded the corner.

"Probably had to take orders all his life, but now, he's asserting himself. The idiot reported me and my father when we were just getting back from the latrine, a couple of minutes late for roll call one night. . . Chee-se."

As they neared the watchtower, George said, "Kim, it's sure good to meet you, and I hope you'll spend more time with us. Maybe, tomorrow after lunch, we can meet at the music room. I'll tell these fellows, and we can have a bull session."

Kim was not sure that he wanted to join them, so he politely said, "Thanks. My old man should be taking his nap, so I'll try to be there."

Chapter 13

Tanforan 3

Oh good! Here comes George, Tomiko thought with excitement when she spotted him approaching with Kim. She was with her friends standing by the fence talking with the soldier. Spotlights lit up the tower as well as the surrounding area, and left very few dark corners.

On the other side of the barbed wire fence stood John McMillan who asked anxiously, "Hey, how are all of you doing? I'm off duty, but instead of turning in, I thought I'd chew the fat with you guys … so tell me, what's 'Nisei' anyway?"

"Oh," said Gracie, "that means second generation. We're the second generation in America; our folks are the first, or 'Issei.' And the little babies in camp are mostly 'Sansei,' or third generation."

"Oh, I get it now. I wondered what they were talking about in our barracks."

"Where? You mean you're stationed right *here*?" asked Tommy, surprised.

"Yeah, down there, by the main entrance," John said, pointing left. "It's set far enough away from any of your buildings and behind a wall, but we're fed the same stuff from your mess halls." He stuck his tongue out in disgust, clutching his stomach and let out a belch. "S'cuse me, ladies. Yeah, didn't they tell you about us when you were sent here as assistants? There are about seventy-five of us, and our guard duties are fairly simple. If you look near the entrance in the daytime, you'll see a flagpole … I'm raising the flag every morning this week. We have different shifts patrolling the perimeter of this place. It's not bad: four hours on, four hours off. We sure hate it when people drive by and taunt your visitors standing in line by the entrance." He chuckled recalling one incident, "The other day, some wise guy slowed down and started yelling at a parked car, and who gets out it but an army officer loaded with stripes and medals. Boy, that really shut the guy up, and he beat it down the highway fast!" Everyone in the crowd laughed at that.

"I hear they're opening a canteen soon where we can buy extra things for ourselves," said Tommy. "Any rumors about that? We could use a few things after we get our paychecks."

"They're paying you? Hey, that's good ... Uh, out of curiosity, what are you getting? Base pay for privates is twenty-one dollars, what I'm getting. And yes, I heard about the canteen too but don't know much about it yet."

"George, Eddie and I are getting twelve bucks a month as skilled workers in the administrative offices," Tommy replied. "Mess hall guys—mostly high school kids or retired men—get eight, and . . ." raising his voice and right arm dramatically, "get this: the pros get a princely sum of nineteen dollars."

John whistled, hitting his head with the flat of his palm. "You mean doctors, dentists, and nurses get only NINETEEN bucks?" he shouted. "That's an insult, for cryin' out loud. It's less than a private's pay! What an outrage!" Angry, he let out a long hiss. "What the heck! Is anything fair? Starting with dumping you guys in here?"

Everyone was silent for a moment, somewhat surprised yet appreciative that John shared their own feelings.

Then, after further thought, John said, "Listen, when I go home next weekend, I'll pick up a few things for you. At least I can find what you want or need that they may not have at the canteen."

"Well," said George gratefully, "We'll put our heads together and let you know the most important things like ink and stationery so we can apply to colleges, or hot water bags for our mothers. Thanks. You sure you won't get into trouble doing this?"

"Nah, be glad to do little favors, guys."

Everyone was touched by this offer. Kim was taking it all in and wished he could feel this relaxed camaraderie and good will they showed one another. He realized how limited his contact had been with his schoolmates compared with this younger bunch of city kids. The small farm town where he grew up was the only world he knew, and the American way of life was something foreign to the people who lived there. Kim realized how this affected his outlook on who he was, and in what directions his life could go. He felt himself wavering about these things; maybe he'd better stay in contact with these kids and not drop them as he first planned. There would be complaints from his father, he knew, but he would keep this new connection discreet, if that was possible—especially about the soldier.

"I think it's getting late," said Tomiko. She looked up and saw Venus already high in the sky and near the moon "My folks will start to worry if I don't get in soon." With that, the little crowd disbanded. George saw her home, then joined the group of young men who were escorting the other girls home.

The weeks rolled by, with the residents staving off boredom-induced idleness by filling their daytime hours visiting various mess halls to see what activities might be taking place. By this time almost a dozen mess halls had been built, allowing the whole camp to have meals at the same hour instead of people lining up in shifts. The rest of the time, these halls were empty and open for group meetings during the daytime hours.

While some people just enjoyed walking around the campground and visiting friends, those interested in crafts toted their small projects to the mess halls. Women brought their knitting or crocheting, while men brought their woodwork, teaching each other what they knew, or sharing their tools. Scrap lumber was easily found in the outlying areas where all sizes and shapes of wood were heaped in piles. Small shelves were the most popular projects.

Although anything from Japanese culture was prohibited, a well-known artist obtained permission to teach art classes in *sumi-e*, ink and brush paintings. He had friends on the outside who gladly furnished brushes, inkstones, stacks of old newspapers, and other art supplies.

The older Issei were grateful to have a period of leisure for the first time since coming to America. Before the evacuation they had to scramble to earn a livelihood in order to support their families on their low wages. Many of them were from the Japanese upper middle class, but it was part of a primogeniture system in which the exclusive right of inheritance went to the firstborn son. These Japanese men were second or third sons, so they inherited nothing. They were familiar with leisure-time activities from their childhood, and in spite of their plight at Tanforan welcomed the opportunity it provided for some enjoyable pursuits. In their worn clothes, and with work-roughened hands, bent backs and sunburned faces they had shed any traces of having led soft lives. However, upon closer scrutiny, some still showed their culturally refined backgrounds in their manner of speech and facial expressions.

One day, a group simply gathered in one of the mess halls just to be together. As their conversations progressed, someone began reciting haiku, starting with the classic about Basho's frog jumping into the pond, a poem dear to

the hearts of the Japanese people:
furu ike ya/ kawazu tobikomu/ mizu no oto

> Into the old pond
> dives the frog and disappears.
> Splash! sounds the water

Each person joined in reciting the poem together, eyes misting as visions of people and places from their past came back to them. During the silence that followed, they felt their spirits lifted, and grateful to be a part of this group of newfound friends.

This chance meeting of compatible souls filled a certain hunger they had not had time to fulfill before. In this racetrack mess hall, they related how as youngsters they would listen to parents and other grown-ups sitting around sipping tea and reciting haiku, one after another. They chuckled as they went on to relate how bored they sometimes got, forced to sit and listen to much of the dry grown-up discussions. A man with a wan smile and faraway look mentioned how he never cared for the *shigin*. Another slapped his thigh, agreeing with laughter that he too dreaded it because his father loved the *shigin* so much that he would start one at the drop of a hat. Shigin is a form of poetry chanted in slow, sustained notes, usually describing the beauty of the moon, the ocean, or the trees and flowers.

A man with the presence of an actor announced he would attempt a shigin as he remembered it, apologizing in advance that he had never done one before. He stood up and moved a little distance from the mess table, explaining that his father always stood up when performing shigin. He assumed a formal posture and stood quietly until his breathing became regular. He then took one deep breath and in a low voice started chanting a long, sustained note, with elongated syllables about the beauty of the moonlight. He held the note as long as he could, then, cut off the word as if to emphasize his statement. The listeners were again transported to moments of a lifetime ago. What made this particular meeting so pleasurable was that any Japanese cultural activities were forbidden in group gatherings at the camp. If anyone outside the building happened to be passing by, they closed their ears to what they had just heard. From this first gathering the group remained tightly knit throughout the remainder of the incarceration period and looked forward to weekly meetings at different mess halls.

Many ladies gladly joined a flower arrangement class that was given by a famous expert living in the camp. Hers was one of the most popular classes because most of the women had learned basic flower arrangement when they were growing up, but had neither the time nor the means to pursue such leisure activities once they moved to America.

George and Tomiko spent a great deal of time together at his office building in the grandstand. She was persuaded to do voluntary clerical work with him, which she did gladly. It gave her a chance to be with this man who was becoming more and more admirable in her eyes.

Other times, she chummed around with Gracie, her old classmate from high school. They sometimes went to the music room where Tomiko played pop tunes, or did her Hanon exercises to keep her fingers in shape. She taught Gracie a few simple tunes, and once in a while both sang to little children who poked their heads into the room out of curiosity. They seldom went to the little park by themselves, preferring to go with the group where they could all talk to the guards.

One day, an older girl named Kay stopped Tomiko outside the mess hall after lunch and asked if she would be interested in helping with a new organization. Even if she was already helping George in an unofficial capacity, Tomiko was still curious and reported to Kay's cubicle in a tiny building to learn what was afoot. She was told that on the outside, mainly at her alma mater UC Berkeley, student activist groups were getting in contact with church societies and midwestern and eastern colleges to admit the stranded college students from the camps. The large network of colleges staggered Tomiko, and she chided herself for not thinking ahead or making plans for her own future.

When she got home before dinner, Tomiko told her parents breathlessly with great enthusiasm about Kay's work. "It's called the Student Relocation Committee. They contact colleges back East, and exchange letters with numerous student groups and church societies to try to get as many college-age kids out of camps as they can."

Her parents looked at each other and nodded, silently wondering what else Tomiko might tell them about this committee, slightly worried that she might get ideas to leave camp by herself.

After Tomiko left the family's horse stall by herself to have dinner with George, her father said, "Well, Mama, we may have to let go of our little girl out into the big world. It's hard to do—especially under wartime conditions—and I'm afraid for her safety."

"It's bad enough when they leave home to go to college under normal times," replied Mama, "but we have to hold our breaths and see how long it will be before Tomiko will be ready to leave on her own. I wonder how much success this committee will have, and where they will place the students."

"I have an idea they will help those who were already in college first, don't you?"

"Yes, that makes sense, and later on, they'll get around to those who were just getting ready to enter college."

This new situation sobered the folks, each exploring the pros and cons in their minds. Finally, Papa said, "We'll have to give careful thought to so many things. I'm glad we were advised to place some money in a bank in Chicago for the day we might leave this camp. That nice Mr. Stockman, the Jewish owner of our house, was so helpful when he used to advise me, and even asked if we needed a lawyer, that he had a good one. Yes, he always stopped and spent a few extra minutes with me when he came to collect the rent. Neither of us spoke English well, but you know," he chuckled, "we seemed to understand each other in our own way. He knows about prejudice from his old country, Russia, where his people were treated so cruelly. He mentioned programs and at first I wondered what programs he was talking about. He said that just being Jewish was reason for them to be killed."

"Oh, how horrible!"

"Yes, such a horror is always for economic reasons when a minority becomes too successful or too noticeable with their large numbers."

"Papa, maybe all three of us might leave camp together later on. Tomiko will certainly be safer that way."

Mr. and Mrs. Araki sat quietly, worried about their uncertain future. Just then, their next-door neighbor knocked and asked if everything was alright and if they were going to the mess hall since it was dinnertime

"Yes, everything's fine here, thanks. We *were* getting hungry, but not hungry enough to rush there for pork and beans," Mr. Araki said as he and his wife stood up, clutching their dinner plates and head for the mess hall.

Chapter 14

Topaz

In September of 1942 the residents of Tanforan—who had been there for five months—finally received orders that they were going to be transferred, but were not told where they would be going "for security reasons." They were told, however (as if they cared), that Tanforan was going to be shut down after they left. George and Tommy were ordered to stay behind to close the camp, which meant that again, they would be separated from their families for a few days.

Although it was unintended, transportation ended up being a much simpler operation for everyone, the residents as well as the administration. In the first place there was no train station to have to go to. The train ran regularly, right next to the south wall of the racetrack for commuters from San Francisco to Los Angeles, and most residents had gotten used to hearing it each day. For this move, the trains would stop near the entrance of Tanforan, stopping traffic on the Bayshore Highway, and the evacuees would be lined up to board the cars until all were filled. The only difference was that for the evacuees, vintage cars were pulled out from some storage barn for this move. The plan was to use a dozen trains to transport five hundred people at a time to their destinations. The cars were dusty inside, with the paint worn off in large spots, and the seats most uncomfortable with straight backs with threadbare upholstery, but considered adequate for the hapless riders.

Weeks before, the evacuees had been told that they could make crates in whatever fashion they could, using the lumber and empty cardboard cartons from the numerous scrap piles around the camp. Many families had stored items from their former homes sent to them, if they had been fortunate to have friends on the outside who had agreed to take care of them. Bulky winter clothes were items to see them through harsh weather that they were not used to. They were also sent old curtains, towels, blankets and sweaters so that the internees could have a semblance of home-like comfort in their new quarters, all of which they appreciated. All these items would fit into the cartons that the camp was willing to send on to their new 'homes'.

The boarding of the trains and the long ride went according to schedule and in an orderly enough manner for the two-night trip. Shades were ordered down, but at one long stop, several people lifted their shades and found that they were in Cheyenne, Wyoming. That started whisperings among themselves. Some guessed that they were going to the mid-west, to corn and wheat farm country.

On the third day of the trip, the train stopped and the travelers were allowed to raise the window shades. Blinking, they saw nothing but scrubby, flat land in the bright sunlight. In the far distance could be seen a line of bare hills. On the station platform, the sign read "Delta," and a friendly soldier announced, "Folks, this here is Delta, Utah. We're about a hundred miles south of Salt Lake City. You can start to get off now and wait for the busses that will take you to your new homes in a place called Topaz, Utah."

Rising slowly, some called out to others, "I guess we went south after that last stop in Cheyenne, then."

"I bet they got off course, and had to back track."

"Whatever," they shrugged, as they stood up and stretched.

Tomiko's family was one of the first to get off the train. What they saw looked straight out of a Western movie: a dusty street about five blocks long lined with a hardware and farm equipment store, a grocery, a coffee shop next to a small hotel, several buildings that looked like Grange meeting houses; and across the street, the post office and an office building. Scattered behind this main street was a schoolhouse, a few residential buildings, and beyond that, a field of low-growing vegetables as well as a grove of fruit trees.

Tomiko stared at the sparse landscape. A woman with boisterous young children exclaimed, "This is almost like where we used to live in California! I'll be comfortable in this new camp." Tomiko stared again. This was all foreign to her. *There sure are different ways to live, and others have survived in places like this.* The woman's little boys were shouting and chasing each other, and her girls started playing jump rope, chanting, "Blue bells, cockle shells, easy, ivy, over." *Why, they're singing the same songs I used to jump rope as a kid!*

The bus ride from Delta to Topaz took only a half hour, and approaching the camp, everyone thought that they were going to an army base as rows and rows of barracks came into view. Miles away, in the background of the bright blue sky, were massive mountains that one of the passengers said was the Wasatch Mountain Range.

Within a month the entire population of evacuees was settled into their units. Happiest of all in their new "homes" were the former horse-stall residents from Tanforan. Some of the more ambitious men immediately began gathering discarded scrap lumber from the far corners of the camp to make pieces of furniture. The women scrounged around also, but found little to enhance their living quarters. They would need to purchase materials from mail order catalogues, something they could look forward to.

"This reminds me of the days when we first came to

this country," said Tomiko's next-door neighbor. "We were living just like this, using makeshift items to create a more comfortable atmosphere. While we were in Tanforan, I gathered all our old clothes and underwear, cut them up and sewed them like a quilt for our new beds. It will cheer us for a little while and make our place feel more permanent."

Mama complimented her for such cleverness and asked her where her family had lived before.

"We're from Berkeley. My husband was a gardener and I did housecleaning. We have no children." The new neighbor pointed to her door, "We are in this room with my sister and her husband, though. It's crowded, but we get along and manage to keep out of each other's way. They told us at the office that later on, we each might have our own smaller places."

Tomiko's mother shook her head, aghast, but tried to muster up some encouragement. "I certainly hope so. We know not to expect special treatment, but still—cramming two married couples into one room is not good."

"Well," said her neighbor, shaking her head. "*Shika-taga-nai.* (Can't do anything about it). I'm glad to have met you. Let me know if you want my husband to build any shelves or storage boxes. He's very handy that way."

George went looking for Tomiko as soon as his family was settled a couple blocks away from hers. At Topaz, he did not have the responsibilities he had at Tanforan because now, a Federal branch of the government, the War Relocation Authority, was in charge of the administration of the camp. This time, older men were working as liaisons between the office and the residents. Many of them had been released from detention centers where men under suspicion were incarcerated. As time went on, more and more were released as "parolees" and allowed to go back to their families. George had more free time at this new camp to be with Tomiko, although she was continuing her work with Kay's student relocation committee. George often went to her office and did whatever he could to help and at the same time, checked to see if any of the eastern colleges might have accepted him.

During the first few weeks as residents of Topaz, Utah, everyone was busy making adjustments to their new surroundings, and getting acquainted with their new neighbors, simply getting used to the new rhythms in yet another camp. The children quickly adjusted to their school schedule, some finding it fun, others not caring for their classmates. Certified teachers were hired, and they followed the curriculum set by the state of Utah. There were several Mormon couples who taught in the schools. They were well acquainted about discrimination, and made serious efforts to encourage the confused young people, giving talks about laws, fairness, and decency. They were also known to be very patient instructors, and the students tried to please them as they faithfully handed in their daily homework.

In many ways the quality of life for the internees was improved at Topaz. Residents felt the need to become at least partially self-sufficient regarding the food that they consumed. Former farm hands gathered to discuss details and choose locations for growing fresh fruits and vegetables for the mess halls. A handful of Okinawans offered their knowledge about raising hogs, and they were put to work on that project. (In Okinawa, pork was a regular part of their diet, much to the disapproval of the mainland Japanese who ate fish and vegetables, serving chicken only if a patient was dying). A committee was formed to set up classes in various leisure-time activities. This time Japanese cultural subjects were allowed, such as their music with *koto* and *shamisen* (stringed instruments) and flute, and haiku writing classes. Artists, in both European and Japanese traditions, were welcome to pursue and share their works. Piano, voice, and *odori* (dance) lessons were also offered by former teachers. As for medical matters, the camp was fitted with the same equipment as in regular army bases, with the addition of maternity and children's wards. Overworked Nisei or Issei doctors and nurses were on staff to care for the thousands of patients needing attention day after day.

One afternoon while standing in the mess hall line, Tomiko's mother overheard a woman remark, "They have been good to consider our needs so that we are able to live comfortably." She hesitated, and added dreamily, "But do you know what I really, *really* miss? … our Japanese *o-furo*." At that, all the other women nearby started chattering at once.

"Oh dear, yes! I've missed mine so much."

"I never feel clean after the showers where the water just runs off."

"Yes, there's nothing like a comforting soak in the hot o-furo."

"Ahhh, how I looked forward to it every night. My husband built ours."

"So did mine, using a heating kit he bought. It was wonderful soaking in our hot tub every night in our backyard."

" We never missed relaxing together in ours every night after a hard day out in the field. "

"You know, if it wasn't for our *o-furo*, I would have left my mean husband!"

Fortunately, that year, the Indian summer seemed to stretch out for weeks on end, and the vegetable seeds that the farmers had hurriedly planted were producing in abundance. At dinner, one night, an old lady folded her hands in appreciation, bowing prayerfully. Before picking up her chopsticks, she looked around the table and said, "Everyone, can you imagine, I am eating much better here than back home. We had okazu (*side dishes*) like this only once a week, but here, it has been three times this week already. On top of that, the expert cooks prepare our meals, and they give us such generous portions."

Everyone heartily agreed with the old woman, said their "*Itadaki-masu*" and proceeded to enjoy their meal.

Afterwards, while walking off their satisfying meal, several young people formed a group, watching the sun go down as it cast long shadows of pink-purple hues on the distant mountains. One fellow said, "That old lady back there, gosh, she must have been awfully poor if she thought tonight's meal was a feast. It was very tasty, true."

"Yeah, I know what you mean," agreed another boy. "We're from the city, and got spoiled going to fancy restaurants now and then. What occurred to me was that everyone is going to be stuck here for a long time because we're certainly not going back home any time soon. I can't imagine just goofing off every day with nothing you *have* to do, can you? What kind of life is that? We're waiting to go to college back east, but for them, it looks like they're going to settle down to a do-nothing life for a year or two until the war ends. Then what? Will they be tough enough once they're released to take up where they left off? I sure hope so."

"Someone should start up an English conversation class for them."

"They wont go, even if they pushed us to study, study, study for college."

"By now, they've lost the urge. I remember coming across several McGuffy readers with Japanese notes that my folks marked in---back in the '20's."

Another fellow added soberly, "Don't forget, some of

us came from very unfriendly towns, so we're not sure where we can move back to. It'll be tough on our folks, so we'll need to be around to do a lot of the resettling. . . We guys may be drafted, that's another thing. Our folks will worry like heck while we're fighting, and this war is getting more fierce both in Europe and the South Pacific. Also, our folks don't know what is happening to their families in Japan. I feel for them. Let them enjoy whatever they can in camp with the others in the same boat."

"Yeah, you notice whenever old folks get together, how they love to reminisce, either about the old country, or about friends and their early days in America. You're right, pal, let them enjoy the leisure they never had. God, how they worked so hard so we could have a better life than they did."

Later that winter, a group of young people wandered over to the general meeting hall to see if anything interesting was going on. The weather had turned cold, and outside activities, even walking around the camp, was no longer comfortable. The mailman had returned from picking up mail and supplies from Delta, dropping off newspapers from Salt Lake, San Francisco and Los Angeles.

"Hey, everyone, look at this," said a girl, pointing to an article in one of the newspapers that she had spread out. . . "Eleanor Roosevelt actually visited one of our camps!" Other girls clustered around to look at the article.

"Ooh, a picture of her surrounded by people like us."

"She's in the Gila River Relocation Center. It's in the desert, and look how warm it must be there, the girls are in their summer clothes in the bright sunshine."

"How nice of her to show that she cares about us."

"It says here that right after Pearl Harbor, she tried

to talk the President out of signing that darned Executive Order. She had several private meetings with him."

"Too bad she couldn't influence him."

A young man said, "And look here, it says that J. Edgar Hoover declared that there was no need to build these camps and dump us here because all the suspicious people were already imprisoned. Even with that strong a statement from the head of the F.B.I., the President didn't take his word, and here we are. Tsk, tsk," he clucked, shaking his head. "Tough luck for the thousands of us."

"Yes, but how safe do you think we would have been if we were allowed to stay in our homes? Soldiers who were killed in action would have had their friends and families come after us, you can be sure."

"In a twisted sense, we are protected *inside* these barbed wire fences from a hysterical mob of angry citizens."

Everyone was silently agreeing that this could very well be true.

"Interesting, that the official reason for her visit to Gila was that there were charges that the Japanese Americans there were given special treatment."

"SPECIAL TREATMENT???" everyone shouted.

"Gila is located within an Indian Reservation, and the Indians objected to the government's sharing plan. Turns out that the area is one of their sacred sites."

"It's just like the government to ignore important things like that."

"Wouldn't be the first time."

"I'd like to get permission to put this article and the pictures it into the scrapbook. There's one on the library shelf, and is worth saving." She murmured softly to the girl next to her, "I think this is a great country where women are allowed participation in government matters. Mrs. Roosevelt goes about with her beliefs very quietly, and I'm sure thousands of us women admire how much she does to make things happen, or at least, plants ideas that will benefit all people."

"I feel that our meeting here today was very exciting. I'm glad that sometimes, our getting together like this can be good. It's sure better than curling up and feeling sorry for ourselves and losing hope."

"Yes, we are thankful for important people like Mrs. Roosevelt and many fearless, vigilant people who keep Democratic ideals alive."

"Yes, and we must to do our part, too from inside these camps. The fellows are anxious to prove their loyalty to America, and tomorrow, they are meeting with a Captain who will be here to recruit volunteers for the army."

◆

PART 3 AGITATO

War

Chapter 15

Camp Savage

Boy, that does it. I'm signing up." George was furious. So was Tommy.

"See the way that white officer gave our Nisei captain a half-ass salute?"

"Yeah, shitty. They have guys like that guarding our camp."

"I can never get used to assholes like him."

"I know, but just keep thinking of all the white people who are decent to us."

"You're right. . . Anyway, the important thing is what we're here for today."

George and Tommy were standing in the crowd as a Nisei captain made his entrance into the camp, and watched astounded as the Caucasian sergeant gave him a half-salute, not even standing straight at attention.

The captain had met with the administration, took care of the sergeant, then moved on to the important mission that he was sent here for, to recruit men for the army. Fortunately for him, his family and parents were incarcerated here in Topaz, so the visit meant that much more to him. The crowd followed him to a mess hall already filled with other young men. All attention was focused on the captain's speech about the army's urgent need for interpreters. He briefly told about the hastily formed secret Military Intelligence School at Crissy Field at the Presidio in San Francisco a month before Pearl Harbor, and that the school was transferred to Camp Savage near Minneapolis when all the Japanese were forced to evacuate the West Coast. He went on to say that men who could speak, read and write in Japanese were good candidates for this task, and that as interpreters their duties became strictly classified. Most of the men felt that they could fulfill such duties as they listened to examples heroic deeds already performed in the South Pacific, mostly by the Kibei with their educational backgrounds in both Japan and America. The men here acknowledged to themselves of their limited knowledge of the Japanese language and culture as compared with the Kibei, and knew that they were going to need intense training to match the skills of those already in the war zones. Most of them wanted to sign up, eager to serve their country even if it had treated them unfairly and classified them as 'non-aliens'---*what in hell was a non-alien? Might as well be 'non-citizen'.* They desperately wanted to prove their loyalty to America, especially in its moment of need, certain that they had the special skills that most non-Japanese inductees lacked for the Pacific fighting zone.

That night, behind closed doors, families of these men who had volunteered were embroiled in discussions with their parents amid occasional sounds of sobbing. For weeks these families went about their daily routines discreetly. Then in late 1942 the men received greeting letters from the Army, with orders to report to Camp Savage in Minnesota.

"Well, here we are on a free train ride again, courtesy of our favorite 'uncle'. Looks like we're getting close to Chicago, George, see all those tall buildings beginning to appear, one after the other," said Tommy. . . "You know, all during this trip, I couldn't believe how good it felt like to be free again. It's like getting out of prison."

"Yup," said George. "Sure hard to believe that all we just get up, go with everyone, no checking out, and walk anywhere we want. Got me to thinking: freedom was an idea, a word that we took for granted, and we didn't know what hit us when it was taken away, but when we got it back, it sure felt like the greatest treasure a man could be born with."

Once outside, following the crowd into the business area of Chicago, Tommy sighed, "Feels abnormal that we can go roaming around like this and there's no soldier with a rifle to stop us. Look, we're right in the middle of one biggest cities in the country, and walking this freely like it's okay, that we belong here."

"Yeah, shows how low we'd sunk under military rule back in the camps. I never want to go back."

The two were amazed that nowhere could they see signs of the country being at war, that people were dressed well and carrying on normally, many with briefcases hurrying from one building to another, completely ignoring the two of them who were gawking at the skyscrapers like hicks from the back country.

"Great not to worry what's off limits. Gotta get used to this."

"Yeah, I need to pinch myself."

"Now, I understand what the forefathers of this country were after."

"Absolutely. We need to keep that idea alive, to never take away an individual's sense of free spirit."

"Hey, wait a sec, I'll get the soapbox."

"Aw, fer. . . quit it. . ."

"Look at all this! Another camp full of barracks belonging to Uncle Sam," said George as the special bus carrying them entered Camp Savage. "And look at all the Buddhaheads! Must be hundreds of us reporting in."

Tommy nodded, unable to stop ogling right and left.

He and George were standing with hundreds of other Nisei men in a courtyard waiting to get settled in.

What awaited the young men was hardest week they had ever known: following commands barked at them; having to reply in a rigidly specific manner; being taught unfamiliar subjects from books with non-English characters; listening to lectures by instructors with foreign accents; and being awakened at 5 in the morning for a long day. All of it downright overwhelming. On the Saturday night of that first week, the entire group barely got undressed before falling into their bunks, instantly snoring away.

"I'm going back to sleep," George mumbled to Tommy who was shaking him. He rolled over in his cot, barely able to open his eyes, but Tommy was already showered and dressed, eager to get away on this first day off.

"Aw, c'mon, George, it's our first free day, for crise' sake. You're not going to waste it sleeping away, are ya?"

"Leave me alone!" hissed George, bone tired from his first week as a soldier. The newness and strict routine of being in the United States Army had been daunting for all the recruits.

Always the restless one, Tommy persisted, "Listen, I've got an idea. We'll go out now, and then come back early. Let's go to that Japanese hostel and see if anyone's sister is visiting; and if not, we'll go to the USO, eat, listen to some music and do a little dancing."

The mention of girls changed George's mind. *Why didn't I think of girls? Tomiko's really gotten to me, I guess.* "Okay, the USO sounds good. Give me ten minutes."

An hour later, the two of them, along with a dozen other Nisei soldiers, got off the bus in Minneapolis. The street was lined with large houses, a few people walking around on errands, and children playing in the street.

"Still can't get over it," said George. "It's like a weekend anywhere in the U.S., when people have a day off and just doing chores, puttering around the yard, or the kids playing hopscotch or chasing after balls in the street."

"Hey, do you smell food cooking? Mmm-mm. Feels real homey."

They reached the hostel, glancing about for signs of any women, but saw mostly men like themselves in uniform loitering about. An older Nisei couple had bought the large house, converted it into a boarding house with bedrooms upstairs, and the whole main floor was like a dining and lounging room. Once inside, they saw Kim sitting in the lounge with a Nisei WAC. George and Tommy waved to Kim, then went into the dining room for coffee and muffins. "Hey, a girl soldier," whispered Tommy. "Wonder where she's from, never seen her before."

As they were finishing their coffee, Kim came in with the young lady. "Hi, George, Tommy, this is my good friend, Eileen. She's in the language school in the women's division." He seemed quite pleased with his companion.

Tommy and George were surprised to meet a Japanese girl who would think of joining the army. They felt awkward and did not say too much after introductions were made.

Kim continued, "Eileen and I went through UC together, and we kept in touch after she was sent to Manzanar. She decided that it was better to be doing something like this rather than wither away in that prison camp.

Eileen was a plain but neat-looking woman in her early twenties, with the hairstyle typical of the women of that time, above shoulder length with curls all around. She looked very trim in her WAC uniform. The boys caught glimpses of her looking at Kim with adoring eyes.

She switched her smile over to the boys and said, "My father really got angry when I told him I wanted to enlist in the language school. He said it was enough that the men were being drafted, and wanted to know why I couldn't stay home and take care of the family. Well, he spoiled me by sending me off to college where I got ideas about working in the business world. My sister who's a stay-at-home type will be there with a younger brother, so I felt I that I really wasn't abandoning my parents. I could have gone out to farming jobs because they're desperate for field hands, but I'm a city girl. They wouldn't hire me in factories or offices because I'm Japanese and couldn't get clearance, so when I heard that they needed interpreters, I jumped at this."

"How many Nisei ladies signed up?" asked George, glad that he'd found his voice instead of appearing dumbfounded and staring at a Nisei girl in uniform.

"Oh, I was told there would be about twenty of us right now. They're going around the camps trying to recruit women, but they're not having much success. They hope to have a couple hundred by the end of a year. Later on, they're going to have me going around to the camps and give pep talks. We women are under a different training program, and are going to be stationed in either Washington or Maryland with our work, all stateside, not overseas."

"Of course," said Kim. "the idea of women soldiers is too much for the old Issei folk."

"Do you know," said Eileen, "my father only hinted to our neighbors that I was leaving camp for a job in Chicago. Some of our friends are too bitter, and would never leave him alone if they ever found out he had a daughter who volunteered for the American army."

"Pretty complex, isn't it?" mused Tommy. "It must be hell for the Issei to have to live in a country that won't accept their traditions, let alone their presence."

"Yeah," said Kim sadly, "My father was so miserable living and working in the farm country." He paused, tilted his head with a distant look, "Thinking back, I'm surprised he didn't send me to Japan when I was younger to further my schooling." He paused, shaking his head and looking down, "Maybe it's because we were so poor that he couldn't afford my boat trip there."

Tommy and George silently compared their own freer backgrounds. Both grew up in a small cosmopolitan city and felt comfortable among their friends at school. They were conscious of not being mainstream, but were seldom made to feel unwelcome anywhere they went.

Eileen had an easy manner that made George and Tommy feel comfortable, and the four compared notes about Manzanar and Topaz, the two camps where they had been confined. The men went on to tell her how hard it had been during their first week in basic training. They had to do rigorous exercises to start out their mornings, then having to concentrate on learning what was practically a new language, with the lessons being taught at breakneck speed.

"And this is only the beginning," said Tommy. "I sometimes wonder if I'm going to pull through. It's a lot of pressure."

"Yeah, we were softies," said George. "Straight from college classes with just some sports during our free time." He nodded his head, "Looking back, that all seems like play now when they have us marching around with heavy packs on our backs. That almost killed me the first few days."

"Yeah," broke in Tommy, "On top of that, it was impossible to stay awake during the late afternoons trying to memorize the kanji words."

"Wait till we finish our Japanese language classes here," Kim said knowingly. "I found out that since we didn't really go through basic training first, they're shipping us to Hawaii and putting us through other training that's as tough as the Marine Corps. They're also going to teach us how to survive in the tropical jungles of the Pacific islands."

Not wanting to talk about further training, Tommy looked and pointed to the men at a nearby table. "By the way, what's that game those men are playing over there? That looks a little like a chess board."

"It's called 'go', and is played a little like chess," Kim replied. "My father used to love that game and taught me how to play it when I was around ten years old. I learned a lot about strategy and placements, and I prefer it to chess. . . I'll always think of my old man when I see a 'go' board."

Eileen heard Kim's voice waver, and said quickly, "I heard that the Department of Defense searched around the whole country for an area where there was no strong prejudice against Orientals, and they decided to try the Midwest. They finally made an agreement with the governor of Minnesota to establish a language school. The first group of students were welcomed by the townspeople—can you imagine that? ---WELCOMED!"

"Wish it was like that back home," said Kim. "God, how I felt we were despised in the farming towns. Don't even want to think about it," he added with a scowl.

"A lot of thought has gone into this whole program, hasn't it?" said Tommy in wonder.

"I think it tells a lot about this country." added George. "How free thinking is encouraged, allowing us to make favorable decisions, sometimes even inadvertently,"

"That's why they call it the Intelligence Department," quipped Tommy.

In the weeks that followed, the men could feel that they

were getting tougher physically, and able to cope with the stringent schedule of their study program. They developed a gut instinct for survival, and gained some foresight into what awaited them when they were sent to the battle zones in the Pacific.

At certain times, studying the Japanese language was familiar and encouraging, but most other times the complex military history and the lectures about attitudes of the Japanese mind confounded them. They found the brief sessions on the religions in Japan interesting from an academic point of view. All the students became anxious to send letters in Japanese as a surprise to their parents in camp.

Mr. and Mrs. Ohara, sat awestruck after reading the letter from George. It was written in Japanese in a fairly fine hand, and it struck them over and over, that this was their own son communicating with them in their own language.

Mrs. Ohara had tears in her eyes. "Papa, I cannot believe this letter is from our George. He sounds like my brother in Japan, the way he uses certain phrases, and I never imagined that we would ever reach this kind of closeness. By the time he was in college, we had so few interests in common, I accepted that as natural, that we were growing apart. Now, like a miracle, he is our boy again."

Mr. Ohara was puffed with pride in his son's accomplishment. "Our George seems so grown-up and strong, and expresses himself like an old-time warrior. He certainly has absorbed what they taught him about the Japanese customs. It does seem like a miracle, as you say, Mama. Who would ever have thought our son would someday write to us in our language? And so beautifully! He begins to feel even more like a son, and I'm so proud of him. Of course, this letter is a little stilted, but he'll come to know that he can say things in a more intimate, family-style manner. I am so glad that we can write to him about anything from now on. Out of this miserable war comes this happy moment for us. . . Strange."

"It is ironical indeed," said his wife, with a perplexed look. "Later on, when the children come home from school, I will show this letter to them, and hint that it wasn't such a bad thing to have gone to Japanese school, and that is what allowed George to serve in this special section in the army." She could hardly wait until her husband went outside so she could relish reading her son's letter once more in private. She wanted to go over the style that he used, where the writer expresses himself differently from the way he would converse. She marveled at how well he understood the mores and manners of the people of his roots.

My dear honorable parents,

This is the first time for me to write to you in Japanese. I hope this finds you in good health and hope the camp life has become more tolerable, and that you have found more new friends. I also hope that Yone and Hiro are well. If you need anything, please let me know, and I can send it from any of the stores in Minneapolis where we go on weekends.

Now, I am an American citizen again and am serving in the United States Army Intelligence Corps. I have been studying very hard. The classes are as difficult as any I've had in college, and they don't wait for us to understand; they go very fast from one unfamiliar subject to the next. We have to study for hours after dinner, and our instructors even come to our barracks at night to help us with our homework.

Then, at five in the morning, we are up and ready to do

heavy exercises or march around for miles and miles. In the afternoons when we have our classes, it is hard to stay awake because we are so tired. The teachers are very strict Kibei who grew up in Japan. I don't like them, but don't even have time to dwell on such matters. Tommy and I are so happy to be in this training together.

On weekends, we go by bus to a hostel in Minneapolis that is run by an Issei couple, and we eat Japanese food. Other soldiers go to Chinese restaurants or to the USO where they dance or listen to good jazz music. By evening, we are pretty tired and welcome our bedtime.

So, my dear parents, I want you to know that we are all working hard with a purpose, filling a need for our country.

Please tell Yone and Hiro to keep studying because this war will not go on forever, and they will have to make plans to go to college someday.

Your devoted son, George Shigeo

Chapter 16

Graduation from MIS

George, Tommy, and Kim were relaxing in the sunshine at the hostel patio on a Sunday afternoon in mid-June. This would be the last free day for them at the language school. Inside and out, the hostel was jammed with incoming recruits from relocation camps in Utah, Arizona, Wyoming, and Montana. It was a reunion of sorts since many had known each other back home. They were finding so much to share about their lives after they had been scattered to relocation camps in various states. The place was alive with the cheerful bantering of black-haired, brown-skinned smiling faces. Inside, there were a handful of women shyly sitting in a group talking to some of the men.

The three friends, along with hundreds of classmates had passed their finals. They would graduate from the Military Intelligence Service School of the United States Army, and nervously awaited their assignments to the war zones in the South Pacific islands.

"Well," said Kim somberly, "this is about it for us . Our last Sunday together."

"Yeah," George added, "from here on, it's the battlefields and the enemy. Who knows, some of them could be our cousins."

Tommy nodded, also in a subdued mood. "Yup, I just realized how safe we've been here, even though the training was tough. Now, who knows, eh?"

"Don't worry, we'll be behind the lines, close to command posts and in contact with prisoners who are brought in, not fighting them," said George. "And get this, if we ever have to go on sorties in the jungle, they are going to assign a Caucasian soldier to stay close to us so our buddies don't shoot us. Sounds crazy, doesn't it?"

Kim, not wanting to dwell on jungle warfare, said, "They should have brought a couple of the prisoners here so we could get actual experience questioning them." The other two agreed. They always looked up to Kim as older and wiser. "I'm not running the show, but that's what I would do," he continued. "Then, our studies would have been more than just book learning." After thinking it over, he said resignedly, "What the heck, we'll know what to do once we get there, especially when it comes to life or death."

"What about Eileen? We haven't seen much of her lately," said Tommy, not wanting to pursue Kim's thoughts. They had so much to talk over on this last day together, they wanted to cover many things before they might become separated again.

"Oh, they plucked her out of class and sent her to the camps to recruit women. I think she's been to Arkansas and Montana," Kim replied. He then went on with concern in his voice, "I sure hope she gets back before we're sent out. She was pretty advanced in her studies, and they figured she could miss a few classes before she graduated. They didn't get as many women as they were hoping for." He was afraid he wouldn't see her if she didn't get back, but didn't want to mention his interest in Eileen to his friends. "It takes certain types to want to be in the army. Who knows what motivates them? Oh, yeah, there are snobs in those camps, and some gals can't cope with the narrow-minded put-downs that are dished out to single women in their cramped circles."

"No kidding, that kind of crap goes on?" asked Tommy.

"According to Eileen, yes."

"I can see that being confined makes people pretty disagreeable to be around, but heck, right now, I'm just worried about myself, that they'll send me to Alaska," said

Tommy. "I'll get my butt frozen off up there. Hey, remember when everyone was worried that if the Japanese won in the Aleutians, they'd head south, attacking Canada, and then us on the West Coast? Imagine the mess---nah, let's not even think of that."

"Rumors, rumors, just like in camp," intoned George. "C'mon, let's go to the USO and get our minds off the war. I want to get one more taste of good old American life before we go. You know—girls, some good food, and good music," he said with a twinkle in his eye." He wondered if they would be able to visit their folks in camp before they got shipped out, mainly to see Tomiko and ask her to wait for him to come back from the war.

As it turned out, the students were given two weeks' furlough after graduation. Kim went to Salt Lake to his family, and George and Tommy to Topaz, Utah.

Back in Topaz, George and Tommy caught everyone's eye as they walked down the dusty road of the camp. In uniform and with backs erect, they appeared to be marching, their youthful strides exuding confidence and determination. Some of the onlookers bowed to them.

Rounding the corner, an old man whispered to his friend, "Look!".

"Those young dogs," muttered the other. "They aren't even officers, they got a stripe or two, they're only sergeants."

"Of course. Their whitey classmates graduated as commissioned officers right next to them. What a slap in the face!"

"And they still choose to fight for the country that treats us like this." He waved his arms around the campground.

"What do you expect? They can't see how they never

get a fair chance, poor kids. That's the way it is for us who aren't white in America." With his mouth downturned, he shook his head, "I stuck it out here in this country so's I could send money to my parents in Japan where they could survive the hard life there."

His friend had the same look of defeat, and his voice was full of malevolence, "I wanted to sign up for repatriation, but knew that we'd be mistreated in Japan, so here I am silently putting up with the life here. If I'd gone back, they might even have tortured my family: that's what stopped me from signing up to be repatriated. Besides, I think people there are starving more than ever. "

The men became quiet, understanding the situations in each other's frustrated lives. "At least when we were on our little farm near Fresno, I felt I was doing something useful, working with the soil and growing plants that didn't check to see if I was white or not. My greatest hope is for a better future for my kids."

"You're right," said his friend. "We made sure our children got good schooling. It wasn't easy for them being taunted as Japs, but they told me that when they got to college they met people from different backgrounds who were good to them. That is the America we knew was here for us, and if our dreams don't come true for us, it will be there for them."

"There's still a long way to go, as you can see from what is happening to those soldiers," the other man said pointing to Tommy and George, "but at least they are struggling on a little higher level than we did … By the way, what do you hear on that crystal set you made?"

"Well, the reception's poor most of the time, but the Americans are beginning to win some battles in the small islands near the Solomons—guess you heard that? It's good we're able to get some outside news from the guys who deliver our mail. When they go to Delta to collect the mail and make purchases for the camp, they get to spend a little extra time to have lunch and read the newspapers, and talk to the town's people."

They nodded to each other and parted, two men with inscrutable expressions, who just appeared to be walking aimlessly about the campground.

When he learned that his son and George would be visiting the camp, Tommy's father arranged a mid-afternoon party in their honor at the mess hall. Tommy made arrangements with the resident mailman to buy cakes and ice cream when he drove to Delta to pick up the camp mail. As it turned out, several ladies from the Mormon church baked a huge cake for them for this occasion.

The mess hall was starting to fill up with friends and neighbors, and Tomiko could hardly contain her excitement as she entered with her parents. George was standing with his family and greeting folks who came up to them, but the moment he spotted Tomiko he excused himself and hurried over to her.

He presented her with a little bouquet of flowers he had bought outside and put his arms around her shoulder, murmuring gently, "Oh, have I missed you! Just couldn't wait for this moment."

Clutching the flowers, Tomiko responded in a shaky voice, "Oh, what a pretty bouquet, thank you. I'm so glad you're here!" She kept her eyes on George the entire time he was with her, and could barely conceal her impatience to be alone with him.

George's younger sister and brother were watching them. "Look, they can't kiss in front of all the people," snickered Hiro.

"What did you expect, something out of the movies?" retorted Yone.

"Nah, no kissy kissy at a Japanese party," said Hiro. "I'm going to be a soldier like *ni-isan* [big brother], and wear a uniform when I get to be eighteen. Doesn't he look snazzy?"

"Yeah," sighed his sister sadly. "But they're going to send him and Tommy to war."

"He could get killed, couldn't he?" The reality suddenly hit the young boy.

Yone quickly pulled his shirtsleeve. "Shh, not so loud, you dummy. Don't worry like that. George and Tommy won't be shooting at the enemy. Don't you remember? I told you they only talk to the enemy soldiers that get captured. C'mon, let's go say hello to Tommy."

Several older women were setting out small plates with pieces of cake, and a man was topping them with ice cream scooped from a one-gallon tub. Little children were standing close-by, wide-eyed in anticipation of the treats to come.

George and Tommy circulated among their friends, going from table to table. The older folk were pleased that the two young men could converse comfortably with them in fluent Japanese. The two generations had lost touch due to the language barrier, but happily that had all changed as they resumed their friendship on a closer adult level.

Tommy joked with the old timers, who were impressed with his newly acquired knowledge of their language and culture. In turn, it stimulated discussions among them about the deeper aspects of the traditions of Japan.

"Hello, Tommy," interrupted one little four-year-old boy. "I want to be a soldier like you!"

Tommy smiled, leaned down and said, "Okay, I can start you off right now." He stood straight and saluted. The little boy raised his hand to his forehead and said, "Yes, Sir!"

"You're going to be a fine soldier, young man," Tommy

said seriously, making the little one smile and run back to his mother.

Turning back to his father's friends, Tommy said, "It's good to come back to this family gathering. It's not home, but it gives me a warm feeling. I feel so relaxed now, especially since it was very difficult at the military school. Everything was so serious and regimented, and they made us feel that we had to be perfect all the time. George and I sure welcome this vacation before we go to war."

The older men were all thinking of the risks ahead, but instead, encouraged Tommy and George saying how proud they were of their accomplishments and their show of patriotism to their country that needed their skills

.

Chapter 17

By the end of the party, the kitchen in the mess hall began filling with cooks and their helpers, all noisily making preparation for dinner, with pots and pans clanging, along with the head cook shouting orders. The ladies quickly cleared the tables of the afternoon's special party.

On the way back to their "homes," Tommy asked Tomiko what had happened to Gracie. He was hoping to see her again, thinking he would get reacquainted with her and see if she was as attractive as he remembered her. Tomiko told him that she had gotten a letter from Gracie some time ago, and that her family had been sent to Tule Lake.

"What! She's in Tule Lake? She must be miserable there," Tommy exclaimed.

Tomiko nodded. "I'm very upset. I'll bring her letter to the mess hall at dinner and let you read it. You knew that all men over seventeen years of age were given questionnaires concerning loyalty to this country, didn't you?"

"Yes, but I never dreamt her family would ever declare outright their objections about being incarcerated. Her old man might have tried to express his opinions about how wrong the government is, and put down wrong answers on that damned questionnaire."

"It's really too bad they landed at Tule," said Tomiko shaking her head. "They are actually moderates, and had hoped to go to Salt Lake City and were filling out a lot of papers. As a journalist with so much knowledge of Japanese-American politics, Gracie's father would have been helpful on the outside, but she gives reasons why they were sent to Tule."

"I'm sorry to hear all that," Tommy replied with sadness, then paused a moment and reflected, "While we were studying, it was all we could do to survive those classes. The instructors came to our barracks when we did our homework at night, and for me, my life was entirely taken up becoming a Japanese native. I even started walking, moving, and gesturing like the old timers—just to go with my speech. Strange, like in an acting class, you know."

"Why, Tommy," Tomiko exclaimed, "Now that you mention it, I realize that was what was so different about you and George. All you need are old-timer haircuts and you'd look like natives of Japan."

Tommy merely nodded. His work was classified and he dared not say more about what he might be ordered to do the following month. Changing the subject, he said, "You know, George doesn't say much, but I know he thinks of you all the time. On our days off, when we'd go to the USO for food and music, he'd mention how you would play certain of his favorite songs better than the band there; or maybe that you liked the potatoes the way they cooked them here. Everything was what you'd say or what you liked. You're lucky, and I'm glad to see my pal so interested in you."

Tomiko blushed, and quickly told him she would see him at dinner and bring Gracie's letter. Her spirits were high as a kite, hearing those few words from Tommy, and knew she definitely wanted to be committed to such a good man as George.

That evening, when Tomiko shared Gracie's letter with Tommy, she wondered if the two of them might meet again … Tommy seemed so very interested in all that Gracie had to say.

Letter From Tule Lake

From Gracie Yamane in Tule Lake to Tomiko Araki in Topaz 1943

Dearest Tomi,

This is the first chance I've had to write to you from Tule Lake. I sure miss you and all my friends from Topaz. This place is a concentration camp, and it's right in the United States of America. I'm not happy about the way things turned out, what with my father and brothers all but throwing away their American citizenships. When the government sent out those questionnaires to all the men over eighteen, I wasn't paying close attention to their discussions, but only remember them saying some things about the army, or the emperor. (How the heck did the emperor of Japan get into this?) I'm afraid that I never got involved or thinking much about their affairs.

Now that we've been forced to come here, my brother has explained a lot to me, and many things have become clearer. Here are the two questions that are going to cause troubles galore for hundreds of Japanese American families for years to come:

Question 27: Are you willing to serve in the armed forces of the United States on combat duty, wherever ordered?

Question 28: Will you swear unqualified allegiance to the United States of America and faithfully defend the United States from any and all attack by foreign or domestic forces, and foreswear any form of allegiance to the Japanese emperor or any other foreign government, power, or organization?

In answering the questionnaire, Papa knew that he was too old for combat, so he said "no" about serving in the armed forces. As for the emperor question, he also said "no" because it would have meant that if we were going to be repatriated to Japan as rumors had it, he would be under suspicion over there as being pro-American, and then be incarcerated; his Japanese citizenship would probably be taken away, and he'd be a man without a country. As you know, the Issei immigrants were denied American citizenship all the time they lived and worked in this country—that's over twenty years.... So he reasoned that by replying "no" to both questions he would hold the family together. He persuaded my brothers to reply in the same manner. Now, we are all classified as enemy aliens and Uncle Sam has banished us to this godforsaken wasteland.

Somewhere along the way, the men here got nicknamed the "no-no boys." They claim that they are conscientious objectors, but the government looks upon them as dangerous traitors. The Quakers declare themselves as conscientious objectors and will not take up arms, but will serve in the medical division once they are drafted. The men here didn't have a choice because only a "yes-yes" response would have given them clearance as people safe to be living in camps like Topaz—as if we wanted to live in ANY of these camps, ha ha. So, that, in a nutshell is why we are here.

What a crummy thing, to be locked away in a high-security civilian prison camp. And get this: There's a barbed wire fence <u>within</u> the campground for troublemakers who are vocal in their objections! The men in there are only reacting as they were brought up to do: to protest, as Americans, against what had been taken away from them without a fair trial. Imagine, living in our own country and being treated like this just because we look like the enemy. From the time we were in kindergarten, we pledged allegiance to the American flag every day and grew up believing with all our hearts that we were Americans. We love this country. It is the only one we know, and look at what it is doing to some of us. I've been depressed for weeks over this whole thing. It sure hurts to be accused of being traitors.

You should meet some of the dyed-in-the-wool Kibei

fellows who grew up in Japan. You know, they were born here but sent to Japan as children because of the hard times during the Depression. Their parents stayed here, working and sending money to the relatives in Japan to raise the boys who were mostly first-born sons. These men are in their mid-twenties, but to me they behave like the older Isseis, even speaking English with that strange accent. They have no use for those of us who have never been to Japan, but they made sure they got my brothers into their clique to attend meetings in a barrack room in the evenings. Papa is pulling my brothers out of that group. At least he came to his senses after observing the mentality of these young men trained in Japan. Mama is relieved, too. Many of the old folks have been living in America far too long to get swept back into any sense of loyalty to their former homeland. He and Mama have always been grateful to live in this country. Personally, the thought of living in Japan scares me to no end. And it's sad to see that Papa can't understand that by just being honest, he became an undesirable "no-no."

At any rate, we're here now. Like I said, though, this is a concentration camp compared to Topaz. That separate stockade surrounded by barbed wire, it was terrible to watch them being herded there, especially the younger fellows who were inexperienced and confused. Someone told me that the stockade is under the jurisdiction of the Justice Department, whatever that means. I guess they live under a different set of laws and are punished differently.

I hear from the old-timers that when they first arrived here at Tule Lake, they established a routine for the people, sending children to an American–style school, and starting baseball teams and a Boy Scout group. At the same time, they were figuring out what kind of labor would bring revenue into the camp. Since there is nothing around for miles, they made a big farm out of these 4,000 acres, raising livestock and using residents working the fields to grow our foodstuff. So many of the people here were farmers before, so the men and women work either out in the fields or in the sheds packing the produce. The internees now complain that we do not get what's being produced here; that it is all sent to feed the army officers elsewhere, and that we get the same pork and bean slop that's fed to regular soldiers.

Prisoners like my family, who only know city life, have a hard time finding work. I've already applied as a typist and a teacher's assistant. Papa used to work at the Japanese newspaper back home, so he hopes to be doing something in the Tulean Dispatch offices as a camp news reporter.

I think they are setting up a war factory to make supplies for the armed forces like they do in Germany, where the Jews work in shops in their concentration camps. Everyone working here will be getting paid twelve to sixteen dollars a month. Doctors, nurses, and supervisors get nineteen. I remember how John McMillan told us back in Tanforan that he was getting twenty-one dollars as a private in the U.S. Army.

The housing conditions here are similar to what we had in Topaz. We're in a long barrack that contains six rooms. The five of us are cramped into one of the twenty by twenty-six foot rooms. Tomiko, I swear, if by some miracle we ever get to the outside, I'm going to make lots of money and live in a mansion with twenty rooms and five bathrooms, and half the second floor all for myself. Good thing my brothers are older than I am and still treat me like a baby, so as a family, we're fine. Mama managed to barter enough empty rice bags to curtain off my "bedroom". She's made friends with some women who get together and do a lot of knitting, and they are all happy that they have enough interests in common to stick together. They say it's going to be very cold up here this winter so they're all busy knitting sweaters, vests, scarves, mittens, and caps for their families. At least we're allowed to send for things from the Monkey Ward catalogues, so a lot of yarn gets delivered here.

Write to me soon, won't you? I want to know about the kids we used to hang around with and what they are doing. Are George and Tommy doing well? What ever happened to Kim? He was so different, and yet so interesting and intelligent. I was afraid I'd see him here as a "no-no," but he must have talked his father into answering the questions the right way and managed to save their scalps.

There are rumors that my brothers will regain their American citizenship. They both talk about going into the army as volunteers if and when they'd be allowed. Being bilingual, they'll be needed at the MIS in Minnesota, and my folks are agreeable to their volunteering to fight for Uncle Sam.

Oh, there's another rumor. The higher-ups in Washington want to close every single one of these blasted camps, but—get this—not until after the presidential election next year. Not good politics right now, they said. By then, the hysteria about Pearl Harbor will have shifted to other horrible things that are happening all over. My brothers are saying how tired they are of being manipulated and buffeted around by a bunch of incompetents.

I promise you I'll answer your letter promptly, so please write. Do you hear anything about John McMillan? Last I heard, they sent him somewhere to fight. I hope he'll be okay. Looking back, those were great times in the early days at Tanforan when we had our bull sessions, weren't they? Even fun. It's so true, isn't it, that all good things come to an end.

Love, Gracie

P.S. Isn't it amazing that our letters are not censored? If we wrote to servicemen with APO addresses, the censors would be right there opening our letters.

Chapter 18

Overseas—Sailing to Hawaii

Dozens of men were sprawled out directly on the upper deck of a transport ship, soaking in the sunshine with the ship steadily steaming eastward in the Pacific Ocean. This was their fifth day out of San Francisco, rocking in calm seas that were considered fairly safe from torpedoes or bombers. The enlisted Nisei crewmen had been allowed on deck for an hour of fresh air.

Some of them could easily have been thought to be enemy Japanese soldiers. George and Tommy were among a group of twenty lying in a corner, with guards nearby. Others on deck wondered about them until they heard Tommy giving George a hard time about their last night in a San Francisco barroom. Both men welcomed this time to "unwind" from six months of intense studying, compounded by the heart-wrenching departure from their parents and friends at the camp in Topaz. It was the first time the men had seen tears in their fathers' eyes, while it was their mothers who bravely held in their sadness.

Always the talkative one, Tommy broke the silence, "Hey, did you see Pop's friend at the gate when we were leaving Topaz? You know, Mr. Toshiya, that usually happy-go-lucky man, who used to walk up and down the streets in Japantown all the time?"

George, lost in his thoughts about Tomiko, didn't want to respond, but to cover his annoyance, said, "Yeah, poor guy, this hit him hard because he watched us growing up, and always came over on weekends after church. Being a bachelor, I think he felt at home with us and that we were all like family to him. Sad that his wife died some time ago. I saw that he had tears in his eyes and walked away sobbing quietly."

"It was pretty sad to leave Topaz," Tommy replied.

Still not feeling talkative, George remained silent, thinking only about Tomiko. He was missing her already, and felt surely that this was a woman he truly loved. She had shown how much she cared all during the visit. Looking over at Tommy, he saw that his pal wanted to keep on talking. Stretching his arms wide, he finally said, "Right before we left, my kid brother spilled out that he knows soldiers get killed when they go off to war, and I had a hard time reassuring him that I would be okay. He's so young,—only nine—and just growing out of being a little child. I tried and tried to calm his fears, poor kid. He kept saying that soldiers died when they were sent out to fight, and I told him I wasn't going to be fighting, that I would be in a safe place, just talking to prisoners who were captured … Other than that, the visit was alright. Tomiko and I had a serious talk and she said she'd wait for me to come back."

"Lucky you." For the first time, Tommy sounded forlorn about someone, George noticed, as his friend rambled on. "I thought I'd find Gracie there. Now, I feel terrible about her family being sent to Tule Lake … Shit on this war!"

"Yah, a lot of shitty things going on all over the world!" George shot back. He couldn't wipe the frustrated look from his face … "Hey, let me just enjoy this sunshine and fresh air while we can. Not all the fifteen hundred guys on the ship get this privilege, you know."

"Oh, okay. Sorry. Are you sleeping much at night? I can't sleep too well with the guys snoring or farting all night, and that kid whose dinner comes up whenever this 'cruiser' starts rolling."

"Shut up, will ya, Tommy."

◈

So, this is Hawaii, eh? George wasn't quite sure what to think as they spotted land ahead. Steaming into Pearl Harbor with its nondescript skyline, they saw empty plots of land— land that had been cleared of bombed buildings. What sobered the crew the most as they stood at the railing of the ship was the sight of half-bombed ships with repairmen working in them. They realized that they were, indeed, on the outskirts of a battle zone. Military men and their civilian assistants were seen going about their duties. There were so many Orientals among them that George remarked to Tommy, "It's like we're in a foreign country in the Far East."

"Yeah, and I can hear them speaking pidgin English. Listen—hear them yelling?"

"Un huh. They walk around like they own the place too. Apparently they must not feel like outsiders the way we were made to feel back home."

"There weren't that many Caucasians living here in the past," Tommy noted. "Far Eastern people were in the majority, not the minority."

"Well, now all the Stateside Caucasians are running this area," George replied. "You know, the officers and the big shots."

"Well, we're almost there now," he said to Tommy. "Feel that heat and humidity. They say that the islands where they're sending us are even worse—more like the jungle."

"Yeah, but the way it is here, I like it," said Tommy. "No wonder people used to come here for vacations; at least the rich ones."

"You can have this weather, Tommy. It's not for me. Too humid!"

The ship docked and all the soldiers were ready to

disembark right away. Each one was wondering what kind of action awaited them, being this close to the dreaded fighting and men killing each other.

Chapter 19

Hawaii

George and Tommy were housed in a small barrack at Pearl Harbor with a dozen Nisei who had graduated with them from the language school. Each working day Caucasian soldiers escorted them to a fenced compound where they did their translation work. At the end of the day, they were again escorted back to their segregated barrack and ate dinner in their mess hall.

The Nisei were officially confined to these quarters and not allowed to go into town on their day off as the other soldiers were. Through the efforts of Mr. Choi, a prominent businessman, one Sunday, they were allowed to go to the USO canteen, although ordered to stay close to a couple of designated Caucasian buddies. Still, they could relax while there, listening to the band, dancing with the local girls, and helping themselves to food and sodas on the snack table. They wolfed down hot dogs and cupcakes, and tried chilled pineapple and papaya chunks, all things they could never get in the mess halls.

George and Tommy were happy to get away from their glum jobs for the day, and really enjoyed rubbing shoulders with the other guys. The two hoped that they would be allowed to return the following weekend. Shouting over the band playing "Jeepers Creepers", Tommy said to George, "Boy, look what we've been missing! This is as good as the USO back in Minnesota, isn't it?"

"Yeah, and in some ways better. Hey, look, that Japanese gal brought a big platter of *onigiri*. I'm going to grab a couple before they disappear."

They hurried over to the table where the girl was setting

down a big plate of rice balls. Tommy, ever the outgoing one, winked at her and asked her name.

"My name is Sadie, or Sadako," she replied. She was wearing a colorful muu-muu with a scarf tied around her midriff and into a huge bow in the back like an obi. Smiling, she continued, "I hope you'll have a good time today. We heard that some of you Nisei would be here and thought you might welcome these, so my mother and I made a batch for you."

Reaching out and grabbing a couple of pieces, George stuffed his mouth with the rice balls. "Ahh, we sure have been missing good old *ogohan (rice)*—so nice of you to make this for us."

Pleased to hear that, Sadie told them, "My brother's fighting in Europe, and he wrote to us saying how much he missed his rice, so Mom and I figured you fellows must feel the same. She also made some *otsu-kemono* [pickles]. It's in that covered bowl so the smell doesn't offend people who don't know what it is."

Tommy quickly finished his plate and said appreciatively, "Sadie, this is a big treat for us, and I'm going to eat more later. But how about a dance with me right now?"

"Why, sure, I'd love that!" she responded, and they quickly melded happily onto the dance floor.

George looked around, hoping to find a good-looking girl to dance with. He saw an assortment to choose from: some blonds, a redhead, and lots of dark-skinned girls with Oriental features. "Hi Miss, this is very nice here" he remarked to a pretty, dusky girl. "I'm having a good time. You know, they keep us pretty busy over there," he continued with a frown, pointing his thumb in the direction of the barracks. "And now I'm ready for something more enjoyable and fun. May I have this dance with you?" As the band started playing "Don't Sit Under The Apple Tree," he took her arm. "That's a good tune. Let's go!"

For George and Tommy, as with the other Nisei, it was good to be able to get away like this after being under great tension with real war work. They had heard rumors about being sent to fight in remote islands, or that they would be transferred to Australia, where General MacArthur was in charge of the South Pacific command. They were puzzled as to why they had even been temporarily stationed here in Hawaii. *Must be stuff going on in those islands,* the young men assumed, since they had heard how much more work was being done with captured papers of late.

The band was taking a break, and Tommy, George, and Sadie got together outside on the patio. "You know Sadie," George said, "where we came from, we've never felt at home like the way we see you do—you look so comfortable like you know you belong here."

"We Orientals are not a minority here, you know," replied Sadie in a serious tone. "There are too many of us to herd around, so instead of putting us into camps like they did to you stateside, they locked up only the ones the government suspected as most harmful, and left the rest of us alone. Hundreds of my brother's friends volunteered gladly and are in the army—the 100th Battalion—but they are segregated. They don't mind that at all though, and say it's better than being thrown in with a bunch of strangers. They felt they could work better just with each other. You know, we talk differently from all you Statesiders. You call it "pidgin English," but even that way, we get our work done good enough."

The soldiers were getting more boisterous, and George and Tommy felt as if they'd had enough diversion for the day. "Sadie, we need to get back before it gets too late," Tommy said. "We were told our curfew is no later than sundown, and I want to start a letter to my folks before I hit the sack.

They sure love it now that I can write in Japanese and they can understand what I'm saying. So, thanks for the nice time, and I hope we'll meet again."

Chapter 20

The Marshall Islands

George and Tommy got off the ship on Majuro, one of the atolls that are part the Marshall Islands.

"This way," said a soldier abruptly as they came down the gangplank. "You're to follow me." He led them toward several buildings in the center of a compound. The two young soldiers were the only Japanese in sight, and they were getting unfriendly stares in spite of their American uniforms.

"In there," the soldier directed them through a door. Once inside, they stood at attention as an officer entered.

"George! Tommy!"

"Kim?" George and Tommy said in unison as they stared, then saluted their friend, who was now a second lieutenant. "Sir," they added hastily, somewhat in shock.

"At ease," Kim said with smile. "Things have been happening very quickly here. I arrived on the island just yesterday myself and hoped I'd be seeing you. I requested the two of you when I told the Navy I needed a good team here."

Not sure how proper it was to comment, both simply said "Yes Sir."

"Your duties will be to interview the prisoners who are crammed into the five tents in the stockade. We've interrogated some of them already, but want to see what other information you can get out of them since they respond differently to each of us. With my rank, I may be as intimidating to them as our Caucasian interpreters are, so I'm hoping the two of you will put them more at ease to open up. I've interviewed one enemy officer, a captain, who is a tough nut to crack. When we found him he was unconscious due to injuries. That was the only thing that had prevented him from committing suicide, and he has been uncooperative.

"We've collected a great deal of their reading materials, as well as the journals that their government encourages them to keep. Most of their tablets are filled with poetry or abstract musings, some of which are very simple, childlike writings by the younger ones. They are humiliated to have been captured, so you'll have to deal with that in order to draw them out. What I learned is that they are surprised to see us here," Kim continued, gesturing to indicate the three of them, "because in Japan the people were told that the United States has rounded up and killed all of its Japanese American citizens—men, women, and children. I do believe we've given the prisoners just enough information to satisfy their curiosity about that.

"There is another matter that needs immediate attention along with your interviews with the prisoners," continued Kim.

Both George and Tommy showed that they were curious.

"The other interpreters have been hearing from these prisoners that thousands of Japanese families have been inhabiting these remote islands for many years. I want both of you to go out in PT boats that will take you to places designated on charts that are marked with tiny islands that abound in this area."

Sensing his friends' discomfort while still standing at attention, Kim pointed to George, and said again, "At ease, George," and leaned back in his seat. "You too, Tommy."

When George found his voice, he cleared his throat and said, "Thanks, Kim; it seems like it will be tough here among not-too-friendly comrades, but we are surprised and feel lucky that you're the commanding officer for this work."

"I agree," joined in Tommy. "We were doing work in Hawaii, and after that were sent to jungle training at a place right in the middle of the island that we never imagined was there. It was just like these tropical islands, they told us. But hey, to see you like this, out of the blue is one big surprise. How have you been, anyway?"

"Things were fine." Kim paused for a moment, wondering where to begin. "I've been doing translation work in Maryland with my friend Eileen. Remember her? You met her in Camp Savage. We were planning to get married last week, but I got orders to come here instead."

"Cripes, Kim, everything seems so farfetched," said George. "Tommy and I were able to go back to visit our families in Topaz, then got on this lousy transport ship in San Francisco and were sailing around for three weeks before we landed in Honolulu. It's kind of exciting in a bizarre way, like an adventure that might happen in our dreams—except that when we wake up we find out how real it all is, and that it's wartime. Alarming too, that this time it's all happening not too far from here."

Kim stood up and smiled. "One more thing, guys. There's a lagoon down there beyond the tents, and the men go there in the evenings. The corporal outside will stand guard whenever you'd like to take a dip, so go there, and afterward get a good night's sleep for the work you'll be doing tomorrow. Dismissed."

Exploring an Island

George and Tommy trudged down a hill in the humid jungle island that was sitting atop the vast blue sea. They could feel the sun filtering through the intermittent shadows of the trees, forcing them to watch their steps on the slippery path covered with rotted vegetation. They were headed toward a stream down the steep slope that they couldn't yet see; but from the noisy gushing sounds, they could tell it was swift and good sized.

Both men were wearing worn-out boots, old pants, and faded shirts—all of indefinable origin. They were not even wearing their dog tags. Their hair was matted and stringy, perspiration ran down their faces and necks, and their shirts were wet and clinging to their backs. Each carried only a machete taken from captured Japanese soldiers. What they hated most was wearing the old clothing taken from the dead enemy soldiers, even though they had been thoroughly washed.

Their orders were to scout for the reported presence of a Japanese settlement that was on one of the islands. The night before, they had been silently dropped off by a U.S. Navy boat from the island base thirty miles away.

George and Tommy communicated with each other only in Japanese, and dared to do so only when the sounds of the stream might partially cover their voices.

"We may have been spotted last night as we landed, so be careful, Tommy," whispered George. "If we follow the stream, we're bound to come upon the settlement if it's on this island."

"Yeah. I want to clean off a little when we get to the water. Cripes, look at your shirt, George; it's all wet, and your pants look like you've peed down the whole leg. Gettin' old, pal."

"You should see YOUR brown pants in the back, Tommy," George retorted, trying not to laugh. "Sure you didn't let out more than gas?"

"We have to use these pills when drinking the water, don't forget," George said as he patted his shirt pocket. He felt his pants pocket, saying, "As for food, this bit of dry stuff from last night will have to last us."

"Yeah," said Tommy seriously, "That's if we survive long enough and get back to that pick-up spot tonight."

They looked at each other, and for the first time realized the thought that hits every warrior: they could be killed. Finality was staring them in the face.

George clamped his mouth to signal silence.

Tommy nodded.

They looked in all directions: above, below, and to the right and left, taking turns glancing backward or ahead for signs of soldiers or natives.

Tommy stopped short, thinking he heard a sound and pointed to a bush ahead. They waited for a few moments.

"*Niwa-tori.*" [Chicken.] It looked at them, squawked, then ran away.

"Good, that means there are people around here—but where? Let's follow it."

The sound of running water got louder, and they could feel the cooler air being wafted up by the stream. The stream in sight, they crouched under a bush for several minutes, watching it for any signs of movement and making sure they were not visible from below. They lay down on their stomachs, and even though the silence made the place seem deserted, they stayed that way, waiting nervously.

"The sun's moved a few feet over; must be forty-five minutes we've been here."

"Yeah, it's been quiet. What say we move along? Let's follow where that chicken went, but first I'm gonna wash up."

They reached the stream, washed their faces and arms and ran their wet hands through their hair. "*Ya-a, i-i kimochi da!*" [Boy, this feels good!]

"Shush, not so loud, stupid."

From the opposite side of the stream, they heard a faint

cry. "*Mi-zu!*" [Water!]

Both froze. Taking a chance, they cautiously approached the sound and listened for any movement, surmising that the voice was truly that of a weakened man, and not a ruse.

Sprawled on the ground was an old man trying to lift his head. "*Nodo kawai-teru ... Mizu.*" [My throat's parched ... Water.] As his voice indicated, the man was too weak to even raise his head, let alone sit up.

George stayed behind, covering Tommy as he approached the old man.

"*Oi, kega shitan ka?*" [Hey, did you get hurt?]

The man was about to faint. In Japanese, Tommy told George, "Water, to revive him."

George picked up a cup lying near the man and ran, slipping part of the way down to the stream. He filled the cup with water and took it back to the man, as Tommy provided support for him to sit up. They raised the old man's head and put the cup to his mouth for a sip.

After a mouthful or two, the man's eyes cleared. "*Un-un, iki-tsuke ta do.*"

[Ahh, I feel revived.] He closed his eyes and snored.

"Okay," said George as he glanced here and there, then whispered in Japanese, "He's pretty weak, and this place seems deserted. Let's leave him and scout around to see if we can find where he must have lived." He beckoned Tommy to climb up the hill with him. "We were right about finding people living close to water. Let's go."

They rounded the corner of a wall of tangled vines twisting upward on tall trees, and were surprised to be in a clearing. They seemed to have entered another country. Ahead of them, a half-mile away, lay a cultivated valley in full sunlight, with crops rotting in clusters. The stream had been diverted to water the crops, and here and there were small trees bearing a strange orange-pink fruit, the size of a golf ball.

"Well," said George, nodding his head, "There was definitely a settlement here." They walked to the vegetable field, picked a handful of leaves, and pocketed a couple of fruits from under the tree, all the time searching for dangers. "Look, over there to the right. The main stream continues its course, and alongside it are huts."

"Look at that,—primitive shacks. Wonder what the story is on those people."

"C'mon, Tommy, let's get back to the old man and see if he's any better; then we can question him."

"They all left in our canoes when they heard gunfire every day and every night. We got to know the bombing schedules. I was too sick, and there was hardly room in the boats. I thought I was going to die anyway, and told them to leave without me."

"Did they say where they were going?"

"No. But I think they were heading for an island that had a lot of caves where they could hide."

"How long have you lived here?"

The old man faltered. Tommy gave him another sip of water and a few vegetable leaves that looked like spinach. The old man chewed slowly with relish. "My favorite greens." He paused again before going on. "We've lived here a good twenty years, over a hundred of us. We left Japan after three straight years of crop failure and sailed to this island on a government ship. Many of our neighbors also left the surrounding village, half of them to other islands close by. Twice a year, we used to get together, once at Obon, and then on New Year's. At least we were not starving, and our children were healthy. We tried to keep them literate with makeshift classes and taught them reading, calligraphy, and arithmetic. Some of us elders used to recount what history we could remember of the old country. We found it difficult to keep in touch with Japan, so this became our homeland.

"After the war started, the army from Tokyo sent their soldiers and took our young men away to fight their war. They even took some twelve-year old boys. Only the old men and the women and children remained, but we managed to keep from starving by tending to the crops and raising chickens and eating whatever we could catch from the sea." By this time, the man became breathless, fatigued from his efforts. He stared into space, then dozed off again.

After another brief snooze he awakened and scrutinized George and Tommy. "Who are you young men? Where are you from? You are somewhat different from the soldiers who took away our men. You do not look like you have suffered in this war. Was your island untouched? Didn't the soldiers from Tokyo find your settlement? Did you go back to Japan for schooling? You both speak well. How did you get here?"

George gave the old man a fruit from his pocket. "Chew it slowly; that's all I have, *o-ji-san*."

The man gobbled it down quickly, burped, and fell silent again.

"Let's carry him back to last night's landing spot," George said. "It's going to be tough through the slippery parts."

He and Tommy looked sharply at each other when they heard planes in the distance.

"Listen, planes coming from that direction!" Tommy exclaimed, his arm sweeping up.

"Quick! Let's go where they can't see us and shoot at us!"

The old man became alert. " Our Navy planes. I can tell by the sound. We used to hide in caves over there." He pointed to the slopes. You boys go—you can run. Go!" he ordered."

"*Un, ombu suru zo. Doko ni ikun kai?*" No, I'm going to carry you piggyback. Now, hang on and tell me where to go."

Quickly, Tommy lifted the man onto George's back and the three crossed the stream and rushed towards the slopes.

"Here," he said unexpectedly when they were halfway up one of them.

All that the boys saw was a messy tangle of branches and rocks. "Nothing here."

"Under that tree. Let me down so you can push the branches aside."

The planes were fast approaching.

The boys did as the old man instructed, and scooped away the branches and rocks. To their astonishment, they uncovered a large cave opening and cleared the opening further. Tommy went in first and waited until George hurriedly tried to ease the old man into it and then jumped in just as the planes were overhead. "Don't bother to cover the opening. It's at an angle so it's camouflaged, and we're safe now," the old man said. "Up ahead are matches for torches. Feel along the wall with your left hand; you'll get to them. Since it's daylight they can't see the light inside here."

The entrance into the cave sloped like a slide, and it took all their strength to help the old man reach the bottom. He was near collapse. Once they could tell they were on the leveled dirt-packed ground, they felt the walls until they came to the matches in well-wrapped layers of cloth and hurriedly lit them. Several torches lined one wall. They lit only one and looked around. This was a large cave, roomy enough to crowd in fifty people. They lay down on the dank floor trying to catch their breath, relieved not to have been detected. Feeling somewhat safe, they lay there listening as the planes circled the area several times before departing.

"They are gone now", said the old man. "They won't be back." Tommy and George listened nervously as they heard pounding sounds outside. "Oh, don't be afraid, it's the afternoon rain. It'll stop after a few minutes."

Making sure it was in fact only the sound of rain, and not gunfire, George stood up and signaled with his head to Tommy toward the far corner of the cave, then whispered, "Those were enemy planes on a mission and might find our headquarters."

"I guess we'll find out tonight if they attacked our base or not."

"Yeah, let's hope our boat shows up for us as planned."

Chapter 21

Grim Discovery

In a good-size U.S Naval skiff, George, Tommy and Kim sat close to each other. Two seamen were rowing, front and back, while the three with binoculars eagerly scanned the island they were approaching. They strained their eyes as dusk began to settle around them.

"There, Sir," said George pointing forward, "Up ahead looks like what the old man told us about." They saw groups of little islands stretched out for miles in front of them.

Kim said, "Yes, these are the ones no one paid attention to before. The old man you brought in told me exactly how to find it. He told me the position of the stars and where these would be." Putting down the binoculars, Kim surveyed the scene. Most of the islets were gentle mounds, while others had jutting cliffside peaks. He then looked at the sky. "Good thing the brightest stars are out now. Wonder how they ever found this chain of islands. Remarkable that they have been settled by so many Japanese farmers after crop failures back in Japan."

"Yes, that was twenty years ago Sir," said Tommy. "The old man said his family settled where George and I found them, while the others who followed were taken to this group of islands, better for raising crops." Squinting and scanning, he added, "Sir, most of these islands seem too small to support human life. We should get to the larger ones where they settled."

Kim's face took on a serious expression. He spoke in Japanese so that he would be understood only by George and Tommy. The rowers were Navy men. "That old man you brought in was humiliated beyond words when he woke up and realized that he was a prisoner of the Americans. Understandably, he felt betrayed, but I kept assuring him of fair treatment as I tried talking to him about things I thought would interest him. He must have been the village elder because he seemed to like the respect I showed him. Another thing, it didn't hurt when I had the medics clean him up and relieve him of the minor pains nagging him here and there. He's still weak, not much fight left in him. It's jarred his pride that he is in a shameful position as a prisoner. . . I made sure he was in a bare room when I left, and told the guards to leave his door open and distract him to prevent him from committing suicide."

George stared, putting his binoculars up to his eyes then putting them down, admiring the scenery. "I hate to say this, but this is beautiful, something like my idea of Paradise. Look at the stars, the way the moonlight falls softly on the hills, and feel the warm breezes. Relaxing, isn't it?" His heart ached as he thought of the last night he and Tomiko spent together in the desert under the stars in Utah.

Kim nodded while Tommy and George continued their conversation. "I thought we had beautiful sights of the Wasatch Mountains in Utah. That gave me some comfort, the beauty."

The tension of being in the war zone, the need to take shelter when hearing the enemy planes droning in the distance kept them alert, always ready for combat or self-defense maneuvers. Some nights, after falling asleep, they awoke breathless with nightmares of being bombed out of their tents.

"Yeah," said Tommy, "that old chestnut about beauty being in the eye of the beholder carries a lot of truth. Trouble is, Nature flashes her beauty any time to anyone who stumbles onto it.. . Gaaaaah, pee-ew! What's that horrible stink?" He leaned forward clutching his stomach, coughing and starting to gag.

"Ho-ly shit, look at that hillside," said Kim. "Bodies. . . lying on the ground! Hundreds of them."

The men stared at the macabre sight, stunned. Against the shore, a bloated body floated back and forth between two boulders, its head barely connected to the body. There was no other movement. The rowers stopped. What if killers were lying in wait for them?

Inside George's head droned over and over, *this is not the movies, it's for real, it's a bad dream, a real bad dream, a real bad dream.* He became dizzy.

After a few seconds of staring, the men coughed to hold down the bile threatening to rise. Some couldn't control themselves, and leaned over the edge, rocking the boat with each noisy retching.

"Men," said Kim, ever the serious leader, but green as his face was, pointed to the two rowers, "Back to the base now. Tomorrow, we come back with reinforcements."

"Aye, aye, sir."

Chapter 22

Pyre Island

Kim and the chief operating officer were standing on deck on the landing boat as it approached the island where the massacre took place. They could see the sun rising silently, turning the incoming tide into a beautiful azure spread onto a white beach.

After passing several islands no larger than a football field, the chief stiffened, sniffing as he sighted the next one. "Gee-zus, did we bring enough gasoline to wipe out that mess? Gagh!"

"It's early enough in the day for us to burn everything and have it all washed away in one or two good tropical rains," Kim replied.

Getting closer to the island, with the stench growing stronger, all fifty men on the boat donned face masks, some gagging and leaning overboard, retching. Two men had cameras and were already photographing the scene as the boat approached the shore.

The hilly landscape was littered with bloated bodies. Seagulls flew about, swooping down, pecking, and flying away with bits of flesh in their beaks. They vied with each other, as well as the rats scurrying on the ground for their share.

When they dropped anchor, Kim was the first to go ashore, followed by a squeamish crew. Men formed a line to pass gasoline cans from the boat to those standing in the midst of the detrius.

"Miyamoto and Ohara, take your men and scout the leeward side of the island. Then report back to me," ordered Kim.

The eight men in the group trudged up a slight incline holding their walking sticks in gloved hands, rifles slung over their shoulders, a knife attached to their belts.

"The air's not as putrid as it was down there, it doesn't get through my mask. . .wonder why., " said Tommy, as he pointed to the top of the hill, where they were headed.

"I'm curious too," said George. "Gawd, look at this." He rolled over a half-buried body with his stick, two blank eyes staring at him. The others poked at the debris lying about: a single shoe, a piece of a torn rising-sun flag, remnants of uniforms, and pieces of flesh from arms or faces.

They were now over the crest of the hill, which was clear of corpses. The stench had not reached here, allowing them to remove their face masks.

Not watching his step as he headed downhill with the other men, Tommy slipped and landed on his butt when a shot rang out. A bullet whizzed inches past his helmet, brushing George's shoulder behind him.

"Down!" shouted George.

With hearts racing, the men lay on their stomachs with their rifles aimed in the direction the shot came from. They had been still for a couple of minutes when they heard a voice calling, "Help! Please!"

"Sounds like one of ours," said George, looking at his team with surprise. "Wonder why they took that shot at us. What in hell is going on, anyway?" he whispered to Tommy.

"Help … fellows!"

George had to make a quick decision. This could be a trap. "Your division and rank!" he shouted.

"We be ANZACs!"

"What - in - hell are they doing in these parts?" Tommy and George looked at each other, puzzled.

"Sirs?" a young scout beside George murmured quizzically.

"Australian and New Zealand Army Corps," Tommy muttered out of the corner of his mouth while George continued shouting orders as he began to get up. "American Naval forces!" he shouted. "Come out with your arms over your heads!"

Shortly, they heard rustling movements, and a ragtag bunch of ten people staggered out of a dugout, three of them women. They were emaciated, with tattered clothes hanging loosely around their bodies.

The last man crawling out of the hole dropped a rifle and raised his arms as the others had just done. "S'truth, we be glad to see you!" He shouted in relief. Then, upon closer look at George, he shrunk back, exclaiming, "Why, you be a Jap!"

"American Military Intelligence," said George sternly. "We are Japanese Americans."

"Cor, just like me cousin's teachers at the uni, learnin' him to talk Japanese to translate. Sorry, Sir!" he said, saluting.

"Where did you get that rifle? Why did you shoot at us, then call for help, it doesn't make sense," said George sternly to the nervous, talkative New Zealander.

"When the Japs bayoneted or gunned down the others, we either passed out or pretended to be dead under piles of dead bodies. Afterwards, I walked around to see if there be survivors, and found these mates moanin' or just comin' to. Sir, I found this rifle nearby in a pile. 'Course, I picked it up. I shot at you because I thought at first you wuz them Jap soldiers come back to make sure we 'z all dead. . . er, those ladies are nurses. They wuz rounded up after a battle and thrown in with us. We found a sort'a natural cave down there," he paused and pointed to the hole from where they had emerged. "Me mate here, Lester, and me went around to look for things we could munch on to stay alive. I found clams and oysters down in the water—even caught a big fish, and we ate some of it raw, like the Japs do, you know, shi su mi, or somethin' weird like that."

The young naval scouts listened wide-eyed, straining to understand the differently cadenced English.

"Form a line single file and follow Sergeant Miyamoto," George ordered, pointing to Tommy.

With the nurses helping to steady them, the ANZACs struggled to get up and form the line. The Navy men flanked them and George brought up the rear, not bothering to train his rifle on the captives. They were all limping, wounds festering, some more markedly than others, and giving each other a hand when one tripped over piles on the slimy ground. There were bloodstains on their shirts and pants, and George knew they were all in a weakened condition, but saw that they could negotiate the short march to the ship. The closer they got to the shore amidst the stench and the smoke, the more the ANZACs struggled with each step.

By that time, enough gasoline had been poured on the dead bodies around the island and set afire. Black smoke billowed from the fires all around, but the sickening stink of decaying flesh and fresh gasoline was overpowering, relieved only by occasional whiffs of the fresh tropical sea breeze.

Kim caught sight of Tommy and George's group returning with captives. He was standing where several Japanese soldiers were crouched with wrists tied behind their backs, staring dejectedly at the ground.

When Geroge's scouting group reached Kim and the chief officer, he reported, "Sir, we have these soldiers who were brought to this island to be killed. They are ANZAC's, including the three women nurses. They said they've been transferred from one island to another during the past weeks."

Kim spoke to George, "These Japanese soldiers aren't saying much, so back at base, you will question them in detail," Kim instructed George and Tommy. "None are officers, as far as I can tell, and since their leader is not with them, this whole scene will remain a mystery for some time."

The chief officer gave orders to his men to spread out on the island to complete setting the fires, while the others supervised the captives boarding the ship. The ANZACs immediately slumped on deck from exhaustion, while the Japanese prisoners huddled in the center of the ship surrounded by guards.

The island quickly ignited into one huge bonfire, barely allowing time for the last two fire starters to jump aboard the ship where the men were raising anchor. Everyone stared back at the dark trail of smoke where they had been, and watched the sputtering human flesh go up in the conflagration.

" 'Pyre Island," wagged a young man from New York to his buddy.

For days afterward, the stench of smoke and burning flesh remained in everyone's nostrils. During the nights, they wakened each other from horrendous nightmares.

Chapter 23

Brisbane 1

George and Tommy were seated with twenty other Nisei in a Navy transport plane. They were with other Naval men that had been picked up an hour earlier from Majuro Island, where they had been on duty for months doing perilous jungle tracking or interviewing prisoners.

Today they were being transferred to Brisbane, Australia, to work exclusively with documents. No more jungle fighting. Several Naval men sitting nearby nodded and gave them thumbs up, having heard about the work of the MIS. With the motor droning it made conversation out of the question, so all they could do was stare out the window at the vast ocean below, dotted with tiny islands in its blue waters.

Cripes, another transfer. Now, it's Australia. I may become a world traveler yet. George racked his brain trying to think of anything he remembered about Australia, and was embarrassed that he knew so little about the country. *Yes, the English had used the sparsely populated subcontinent along with nearby tiny Tasmania for a penal colony. Was Charles Dickens sent there, or did he spend time in a debtor's prison in England? What a shameful way to treat a national treasure … The natives in Australia were very primitive, black-skinned, and called Micronesians. They most likely lived as our American Indians used to in their own land.* He remembered seeing pictures of them in the National Geographic magazines. *And was it called, the "outback"? The land that was vast, wild, and undeveloped—home to guys like our old cowboys who roamed, lived, and worked off the land. . .* He wondered how backward the country could be, and how he and other MIS boys would be received there. *Oh, yeah, that New Zealander kept calling us Japs, but he didn't say it the way people did back home.* His thoughts rambled on and on.

Brisbane. That's where the men were going, but George didn't even know exactly where Brisbane was. From his seat, he could barely hear one guy saying that it was south of the equator on the east coast, and that the climate was moderate. *Good, doesn't sound like steaming jungles. And what was that talk about MacArthur? Oh, yes, the general had been transferred from the Philippines, and made Brisbane the headquarters of the Pacific war zone . Does that mean that the MIS translators would actually see General MacArthur sometimes? … No sense guessing about any of this.* George was lulled into dozing like the other fellows, only to be rudely awakened when the plane thudded down in a vast airfield an hour later.

Marching to the barracks, George stole glances to the right and left, unable to suppress a broad smile when he looked down. *My god, a real cement road!* There were multi-story buildings everywhere and no barbed-wire fences. It was like any normal city: plenty of trees, houses everywhere, and in the distance, towers of a bridge, like the one in San Francisco. He was elated. This was truly back to civilization. No more snakes or small critters crawling underfoot, no more flying insects, and no more endless slippery hills to have to trudge. Man had created this predictable landscape, and he welcomed its familiar sense of order.

Once inside their barrack the men dumped their duffle bags onto cots. George and Tommy chose ones next to each other, and looked around the room. Forty beds, twenty against one wall and twenty on the other side, all neatly made, footlockers at the foot, with a comfortable aisle for two to walk through. This time the Nisei happened to be together in the same building, not intentionally segregated as in Hawaii, but simply under a practical arrangement because they were all going to have the same work schedule.

"There will be five hundred of us working here eventually, with more coming in later," Tommy announced. "We're one of the early groups."

"Yeah, that's what I heard, too," George replied. "Did you see all those other barracks, just like our evacuation camps—some life huh, traveling from one camp to another?"

"You can say that again. Uncle Sam must think we only like camps."

"Boy, how much hotter does it get here anyway? … whew!"

"Well, what is it—November? It's summer now," said Tommy, wiping the sweat off his brow. "At least, they've got a fan in here."

Just then, a corporal came in, loaded down with a canvas bag full of letters. "Mail call!" he shouted as everyone rushed toward him.

The men sat on their new cots, a couple of them lying down, reading their mail. George was concentrating as he read a letter from Tomiko, and it felt strange to be hearing from her. She seemed so remote and foreign, even if she was the girl waiting for him back home. It had been weeks since he'd received a letter from anyone. He had been too involved with surviving in the jungle, dodging its unpredictable trails, or on other duties, drawing out information from reluctant prisoners. And then there was the chore of writing out endless reports afterward.

He was glad Tomiko was safe living in Chicago now with her parents. Safer than in Europe, where cities had been bombed or invaded, with their populations having to fight off marauding soldiers who had turned into beasts. He wondered why savagery rose to the fore in ugly shapes within the human psyche when constant acts of violence were so pervasive. Shaking off such musings, he started reading Tomiko's letter.

Dearest George, (Ahh, the tenderness of these words written in a feminine hand—how he had missed this. He felt a slight jolt when it dawned on him that she was writing from another world, so far away.)

It has been ages since hearing from you. I think of you often while sitting in my classes at Roosevelt College, or at a collection agency office where I am doing part-time work to pay for my tuition. It is freezing in Chicago, and I'm amazed that people in the East go through this every winter. Guess what? All the working women wear fur coats! I used to think only rich people owned them, but everyone here really <u>needs</u> *them.* (George could hear her give a child-like giggle at this.) *What a topsy-turvy world we live in, with summer and winter at the same time.* (I love the way she slipped in that she's figured out I'm south of the equator.) *When we were in camp, we didn't know that Americans on the outside were going through another kind of hardship. Coffee, sugar, butter, meat—even shoes and gas are scarce. We need ration books to get these things, if we can even find them. Of course, if we eat in restaurants, we see more variety, but who has money for eating out? People here don't seem to mind because they love things like oxtail soups and scrapples, just drooling over them. So in the Midwest, they say the food shortage is not as bad as it is on both coasts! I've made a few girlfriends at school. I don't tell the Caucasian ones about camp because they are not prejudiced against Orientals, to start with, and it's too much trouble to explain things to them. Besides, I don't want to dwell on those awful days right after Pearl Harbor. There are a lot of us from camp living in Chicago. Some are live-ins in Evanston, a wealthy suburb where people can afford servants . This is a big city, and one Sunday we treated ourselves and rode around in a bus, sightseeing like tourists. Lake Michigan is huge, and reminds me of the ocean along the California coast. We are in a big apartment, but don't have much furniture. It's too expensive, and hard to find. Mama and Papa are employed in some factory working side by side with Negroes who came up from the South to earn more money than they ever saw before. I have to laugh when I hear my folks telling neighbors in a slight Southern drawl about what streetcars they take to get to work, or where they have to go to get Japanese groceries. It's so funny, the combination of their accents on top of the Southern drawls. The employment situation is good, and it is easy for us students to get part-time jobs. Some Issei men and women with sons in the army got clearance to do war work, and are making good pay. We don't go to church, so we haven't met too many Japanese people, but I wanted you to know that we love the freedom of this normal life. Uh-oh, I'm running out of space. Take care, and know that I look for the day you will be coming home. Always, Tomiko.*

Folding the letter carefully, George stared into space, loneliness creeping into his heart. No wonder, he thought, a certain special woman is called your "other half."

Chapter 24

Gracie

Tommy also lay on his cot getting ready to read his mail. He carefully tore open the envelope with Gracie's return address, surprised and pleased that she would write to him.

Dear Tommy,

Tomiko gave me your address, and I hasten to write to you. I hope you are okay. We're so proud of you and George. To bring you up to-date about our family, we were released from Tule Lake six months ago. What a horrible place that was, and I'm so glad that the camp nightmare is behind us. Dad finally got his clearance, as did my two older brothers. They both had their American citizenships restored, and are training at Fort Snelling like you did, but my younger brother is still at home finishing high school. A lot of us Japanese moved here to Salt Lake City from different camps. Still others had moved here voluntarily before the evacuation. We didn't have money for that kind of move. Anyway, the people who were already here were very helpful to us when we arrived. Dad is working at a local newspaper and is also getting involved with the JACL, which keeps him very busy with heavy political stuff that I don't understand. We are in Mormon country, and I'm learning that they have quite a history themselves, fleeing from one part of the country to the other, unwelcome because of their religious beliefs. They finally were able to settle here, where in those days, Utah was the middle of nowhere. They built a huge tabernacle, and our family went to a concert there which was absolutely breathtaking. Imagine, 6,000 people in the audience, all of us thrilled and listening to the wonderful orchestra and choir ... I'm taking classes at Westminster, a small college, studying English and home designing. Also, learning secretarial skills while I work at the school office, which helps toward my tuition. Mom found a job, and we go grocery shopping with our ration books on weekends. I saw Kim one day. He was passing through, visiting his mother who lives down the street. His father died in the hospital a year ago. He said that he saw you and George. If you like, I can write to you again. Stay well.

As ever, Gracie

Tommy smiled to himself. Gracie was part of the original gang at Tanforan. He remembered how the group of fifteen to twenty young people were always together, sometimes talking to the guard in the watchtower, or sneaking into the room with the piano to listen to Tomiko playing the latest tunes, or dance to them, or the men would hold bull sessions about politics while the girls chatted away. Tommy always liked Gracie, but thought she was somewhat flighty, though enjoyable enough with her bubbly good nature. He appreciated her seeking him out and sending him this nice letter that cheered him unexpectedly. If she saw Kim, he might have given her some idea where he was stationed. Smart girl, he thought, to mention very little so the censors wouldn't black out any part of her letter.

After that, Tommy finished reading a couple of letters from his parents. *Well, I hate to admit it, but one good thing did come as a result of this cursed war. I get that wonderful sense of intimacy with my parents that I can enjoy with them as an adult.*

After the uncomfortable noisy flight in the transport plane, and anxiety about the work he would be doing at this base, he felt a true sense of relief that he was back where he could take normalcy for granted. He dozed off, feeling safe for the first time in ages. The room soon began to sound like a frog pond, with different pitched snores responding to each other.

"Look at this," said George to Tommy the next morning as they walked into a huge, well-lit barrack.

"What the heck? It's like we're back in Minnesota," complained Tommy. They glanced all around the room that was lined with double rows of desks, about a hundred of them amply spaced. It was like a classroom: impersonal with an air of expected efficiency.

"We're supposed to be working as a team, so let's go down there in front like they told us," said George.

"Yeah, something about being in a team of ten men to translate documents that were found on captured prisoners, and later, we have to talk to those prisoners."

"Some of them were injured and are still in the recovery ward."

Thus began a routine that was to continue until the end of the battles that were fiercely raging all around them in the South Pacific.

The MIS men spent their weekends in downtown Brisbane as part of a huge crowd of uniformed Yanks out to enjoy themselves in restaurants or pubs where local men and women entertained them with good food, booze, singing and dancing. George and Tommy marveled at the big city atmosphere with its business-like pace, even if they could not easily adjust to the high humidity, or seeing vehicles driving on the left side of the road. These translators felt comfortable, and were thankful to melt into the crowd in one of the largest and busiest military centers, where the mood was winning a war rather than picking them out just because they were Orientals.

After a year and a half into this work, George and Tommy's team was called into an empty conference room. That was unexpected, as well as unnerving. An officer stood in front of them and said they were making changes. They wondered what gross errors they must have made.

"Men, all of you are doing a fine job with your translations and interrogations of the prisoners. We have been satisfied with your work all along, and know that your academic backgrounds are exceptional. All of you are college graduates, or were about to graduate, and your results have been excellent. However, among the new recruits, we have younger men straight out of high school with low academic leanings. Their work, whenever double-checked by others is often inaccurate, some times with glaring errors. We've decided that we might fill the gaps in their limited abilities by adding some basic review work.

"Starting next week, for six weeks, we are going to try an experiment. You decide among yourselves the various methods you can use: individual tutoring, roundtable discussions, or whatever you think will help. We believe with some refresher-type of training, these young recruits may improve. Otherwise, they will have to be transferred to combat duty."

After the officer left the room, the men sat in silence before airing any ideas.

George raised his hand when no one spoke. "I did some teaching in college, but it was all classroom work. Suppose we start out by holding an informal group meeting to see what these kids know and how they think, and then take it from there?"

"Yeah," said another translator. "I noticed how confused and uncomfortable these kids appear to be, what with being thrown into camps in their teen years and exposed to too many rabble rousers. A lot of them weren't mainstream Americans to begin with, growing up in Japanese ghettos, and I'm sure they were taunted as Japs." He suddenly slapped his hand down hard on the table, frustration all over his face. After catching his breath, he tried to continue with control, "We were fortunate to be among people with higher aims when we got to college. Not a perfect world—just a more enlightened group of people we associated with within those halls of learning. That made it possible to cope with the redneck atmosphere on the outside, which is pretty much all these kids knew."

Another fellow, Mits, raised his hand and said, "I know how rough it was for them. We lived on the outskirts of Oakland, which was rural. My uncle was a fanatic pro-Japan character, and he and my Dad argued all the time until they stopped talking to each other. At home, we had lots of unhurried talks around the dinner table, something those kids couldn't have in the camps. I think that we need to give them a broader view of the situation we're all trapped in, and let them know that they aren't the only ones who are victims of prejudice. We should talk about the Jews in Europe, and the caste system our folks lived under in Japan."

One older fellow, Jiro, got up and said, "That's a good idea, very good. We should keep in mind that since they're so young, we'll probably need to build up their self-confidence too. Do you realize that most of them are barely twenty years old?"

Tommy raised his hand and said, "I wanted to become a teacher after I graduated from college, and this assignment will give me a chance to try out some theories that I've got for remedial work. Also, if these kids need counseling, I can do that too,—just a few words here and there. Yup, this'll be good practice for me because I love to work with kids."

Walking back to the barracks the men agreed how disturbing it was that there were serious errors cropping up in their group work. "How did these kids graduate from the language school? Guess they learned by rote and got by," said Tommy. "I feel sorry for them. We know that they didn't have normal childhood years and grew up in a prison-like atmosphere. No wonder they're buckling under pressure. Heck, we had good teachers who gave us special attention when were growing up, like Mrs. Potter. She told us about her trip to Europe one summer, bringing back tons of pictures to show us how people there lived, and it made them so real to us. She opened the world for us, and told us we could go to college, always pointing out the different things we could study there."

George also thought back and agreed, "That's right. Yeah, I remember Mrs. Potter. And it's true, she did take us out of our little world so we could see what life and people were like in other parts of this big world." He nodded slowly and with a faraway look, recalling his childhood days, "And I remember like you do, how she constantly talked about all of us going to college, like it was the most natural thing to do when we grew up … How do we ever thank people like her?" All the others nodded in agreement, realizing that they also had mentors who guided them with such understanding care.

At mess hall that night the team sat together and casually observed their future charges. "Interesting how they cluster together—see them over in that far corner?" said Jiro. "Maybe we should start now and go talk to them."

"Let's hold off for now," suggested Tommy, "and just start by greeting them when we pass each other in the hallways, so's to let them feel that we 'old men' are showing an interest in them."

Jiro and others flinched but said nothing, all frantically wondering how best to comply with orders, and worrying about the heavy responsibility they were now under. If improvements showed up, fine, but if not—even for one man—it meant an enforced transfer to a fighting unit.

Chapter 25

Agitato

Marissa and Charlie,

Here is my last stint as a storyteller. It goes beyond the evacuation and camp periods because I felt that a fuller coverage of what happened could help understand what your family went through during WW II. Writing about the wartime helped me to see things more objectively about a period when we were swept into another way of life.

"Well, here we are, floating homeward in this tin can," sighed George. "Is this a reward vacation, or what? Take a look at that bunch of guys playing poker, card sharks talking about going to Las Vegas and getting rich."

"Lots of luck. Dream on, you suckers," Tommy said under his breath.

The two were on deck, making their way past scores of soldiers idling away the time on an Army transport ship, waiting to get home. There must have been well over a thousand of them, swarming around on its three decks, undoubtedly relieved that there would be no more kamikazes, torpedo attacks, or orders barked at them. George and Tommy were additionally relieved that there would be no more killing other guys who looked like they did. *We're no longer the enemy,* George thought, with a tinge of bitter irony.

The war was over. Europe lay in rubbles, its cities and landmarks destroyed beyond recognition. Poverty-stricken Russia and China fared even worse. And in Japan life had all but come to an end. The country was crippled. In Okinawa people had hid in caves, been shot when sneaking out to get water, and thousands of women and children had been ordered to jump off cliffs rather than be captured. Tokyo had been devastated by dreadful fire bombings. And most gruesome of all, Hiroshima and Nagasaki had been obliterated by the atom bombs that vaporized their citizens.

'We'll be lucky if we get back to California in a month," said George glumly. "We just seem to be floating in one spot, a boatload of us in the middle of the sea ... Christ, the Pacific Ocean is big, isn't it?"

"Yeah, and after we left Australia, we made milk runs from one tiny island to another, picking up these guys," Tommy replied quietly. "Pissed me off at first when we had to wait around a few extra days in Hawaii, but then they gave us shore leave. It wasn't so bad, was it, rushing to the USO to be with those girls who took us to a Japanese restaurant to eat *otsu-ke-mono* [pickles], sushi and tempura? A nice change from the slop they give us here ... Hey George, you seen any of the MIS team that we worked with?"

"Nope, haven't seen a familiar face yet. A lot of the older guys stayed on because of the financial security, you know. That way, they didn't have to go job-hunting. Well, they can have the Army! I've done my duty," said George. Then, with a disturbed expression, he continued, "Besides, there were things I never liked. Like when we graduated back in Minnesota, our Caucasian classmates graduated as commissioned officers and we came out only as sergeants or warrant officers—and you notice, we-still-are!"

Tommy started to bristle, and pounded his closed fist on the other open hand. "Yeah, this whole deal was total bullshit. Good thing they kept us busier than hell, so crap like that was unimportant. Remember back in Brisbane, when we were working on captured documents and figured out the complex messages, we had to turn them over to our white superiors and they got the credit and promotions. They told us that our work was highly classified, so we were never mentioned in the official reports. Like we were nothing."

George put up his hand and shook his head, "We had a backer, though—a most important one—General Douglas MacArthur. He'd worked in the Philippines for years and understood the Oriental people. He always told other officers who doubted us how valuable we were."

"No sense in getting worked up," said Tommy, who was still seething. "Toward the end, they kept telling us that our work helped to shorten the Pacific war by a year or two."

"If that's true, I like to feel that we might have spared even one life, whether it was one of our guys or even one of the enemy's," George said somberly.

Over and over they told themselves no more jungle warfare, no more suffocating heat, no more talking to the humiliated Japanese prisoners who all wanted to commit suicide for having been captured and letting Hirohito down.

During the following two weeks, counting the days, George and Tommy settled down a little and began reflecting. Their self-analysis told them that combat had made them barbaric, almost feral; they wondered how they would be able to conduct themselves in a more civilized atmosphere where the presence of women would refine and soften the coarseness they had developed while in the all-male military society. Some of the other men were anxious to talk about things that had happened on the battlefield, and to relive harrowing incidents where they missed being killed, or saw fellow soldiers taking bullets that could have blown off their own head. These men felt compelled to tell each other about the anxieties that kept haunting them whenever they were alone. Since the MIS men were sworn to secrecy about their work they cleverly told sparse stories about finding enemy remains in caves all around the small unnamed islands, or amusing anecdotes about stumbling about and getting lost in the snake-filled jungle.

The ocean voyage took a month in calm seas and acted as therapy for frayed nerves. With each passing day, many of the men found compatible souls with whom to share the fears and threats they'd known on the battlefields. It helped to whisper to a fellow warrior how petrified they had been during combat, sobbing for their mommies like little boys, with shit running down their pants— memories like this they thought they would never, ever, utter to anyone. Many nights, men could be heard having nightmares, thrashing and moaning in their sleep and awaking others who were in no better shape.

When their ship docked in Los Angeles some of the guys knelt unashamedly to kiss the ground in front of a crowd of civilians who had come to welcome them. George and Tommy watched and wished they could be as openly demonstrative. "You know, I feel the way they do—just as deeply—but I guess I'm too inhibited," said Tommy.

"I know what you mean," George agreed. "Maybe it's our reserved Japanese upbringing."

They each looked skyward, took in a deep breath of America, and then with their hands over their hearts, bowed their heads for a moment.

Neatly dressed in uniform, George and Tommy took a last look at the huge ship and said goodbye to the men they had became friendly with during the voyage, then boarded an Army bus to the train station. In a haze, they stared out the bus window and felt the weight of war being lifted, now that they were back on American soil where the buildings and people appeared untouched by horrors they had seen. The sounds and smells even seemed unchanged from the old days.

The two felt as if they had been somersaulting through a bizarre adventure, and were elated to be standing on the good earth, solid and reassuring under their feet.

They boarded the train for San Francisco, where they would start searching for rental houses to start new lives with their families. The government paid twenty-five dollars to every single person leaving the internment camps, and provided train tickets to their destinations. That meant that their families would have one hundred dollars each in their start-up funds. Some Japanese American returnees faced angry mobs in their former hometowns, and fled to Los Angeles where they sought safety in numbers, but George and Tommy's families were assured by their Caucasian friends of help during their resettlement.

Towards evening, approaching San Francisco, George and Tommy enjoyed a beer in the dining car before ordering their dinner. George leaned forward, lifted a finger, and told Tommy to start watching the landscape carefully.

"Why? What for?" asked Tommy impatiently. "Nothing but empty lots and a bunch of rundown houses here and there. Are you nuts?"

"Just be patient, pal … Okay … now! Look to your right. Quick!"

"Just a low cement wall. Christ, what's the matter—Oh-ho! **TAN-FOR-AN!**"

"Yup, Tommy, Tanforan. Remember how we'd hear this train go by every night when we were locked up in there?"

"And wish like mad that we were free and going somewhere nice … "

"We're getting that wish now."

"Even with the windows closed, I'm starting to smell horseshit," Tommy said, sniffing and staring out.

"They took down those barbed wire fences," added George. "But keep looking, Tommy … I swear, I can see a whole bunch of young people walking toward a certain watchtower overlooking a little park … at the end of the day, just like now, when the sun is setting."

After a few moments of reflection, they raised their glasses silently.

[Someone… Go tell Thomas Wolfe that you CAN go home again.]

Marissa and Charlie were silent after reading the story, Marissa with tears in her eyes, and Charlie deeply moved, holding her hand.

"I'm so angry about what this country did to Papa and our families. In fact, to anyone who looked like I do. Why, I could have been imprisoned, too, if I had been born then. Times have changed. I was never taunted as a Jap, and I always knew that I belonged, especially in New York."

Charlie stood up and started pacing, "Now you understand why I wanted to change majors and become a lawyer when I found out about this. It's a grim story your dad's kept hidden all these years. It really depicts how people thoughtlessly destroyed each other and how that churned the ugliness in everyone. Until now, never a word from your father to either of us or anyone else … Unbelievable!"

"You know, I'm so grateful that I grew up seeing my father in a respected circle of specialists, and as one of them. I want to write to him and thank him."

"So will I, Hon. A few historical questions have come to me, like if he knew about any dissenters and if so, what happened to them. I hear there were three. Yes, your dad is the perfect one to discuss this with. Looks as if we're not finished with stories of that war yet."

Marissa stood up, cradling the pages of her father's

story and thinking. *Papa's finally opened up and now I can see him in a different light. He was a remarkable individual. And Mama, ever patient and quiet in the background. I feel so guilty for looking at both of them as old fuddy-duddies. Turns out I was the one who was so stupid. . . No wonder the old sages were forever hammering into the young people that they must respect their elders. I need to turn a new leaf, and will write to them as a friend rather than as their little girl.*

◈

PART 4 CODA

Andante Cantibile
Back to Life in Las Vegas

Chapter 26

Las Vegas, Nevada, A Monday in August, 1987

For six years Charlie Lyons had doggedly awakened on Monday mornings, ready to teach Nevada history. On this Monday, however, before even opening his eyes he knew there would be no class. There wouldn't be for an entire year.

Huzzah! He was on full sabbatical.

Should he indulge himself and stay in bed, or enjoy a leisurely breakfast with his wife and little boy? He heard them in the kitchen, and their cheerful voices warmed his heart.

He was certain that having Marissa and Lennie in his life had enabled him to develop as a stronger, more thoughtful and mature man, as well as a caring husband and father, Charlie told himself. He was aware that he left a great deal of the household and parental duties to his wife, and realized now that working women truly did double duty. He felt a pang of guilt when he realized that he, like most men, tended to snub household work as beneath him. Often, he would see Marissa finish little chores before going to bed so that she could start the following day with a clean slate, and told himself that at least he handled much of the heavier work and big projects that needed to be done.

While in the shower, hundreds of images flashed through his mind: his first days in the Las Vegas Strip hotel bands, meeting Marissa, her encouragement while he studied for his doctorate, their marriage and birth of a son, to memories of the myriad activities at school, in both the history and music departments, then on to the years of teaching. Once in a while faculty was hired for teaching in more than one field of study, and he felt fortunate to be there at a time when the university was willing and able to offer this diversity in teaching duties. It allowed him friendships in both departments, with the history geeks and the dreamy, artist-musician personalities. He also played in the university's symphony orchestra as part of his contract. Dividing his time between subjects closest to his heart was a very satisfying situation not many enjoyed. Other thoughts ran through his mind as well, causing him to smile. No arch enemies as often happens in the work place. Of course, this was not a USC or Stanford, but as long as he upheld a high standard of excellence, he was being true to himself.

After dressing in comfortable old clothes, he joined his family in their large country kitchen. *Cripes, what a mess— globs of yogurt and pieces of toast all over the table and floor.* Lennie had eaten a satisfying meal.

"Good morning, everyone," he said with a big smile as he walked in.

"Daddy!" shouted Lennie, studying his father. "How come you're not dressed up?"

"Good morning dear," Marissa said. "I thought I'd let you sleep in."

"When I got up, I couldn't believe I didn't have to rush out to my classes. It took me a few minutes to realize it's going to be a different routine. Starting today!"

"Daddy, how come you don't have to go to school, but I do? That's not fair!" whined Lennie.

"Well, let me tell you how it works, Len," said Charlie indulgently as he hugged his son and sat down. His heart swelled with love and pride as he started to explain, "My school thinks we professors need an extra vacation now and then. Not to play, mind you, but to study more so we can let our students learn about the new things that we found out."

Quizzically, Lennie tilted his head and asked, "Don't you know everything by now, Daddy? I thought you were real smart."

Charlie gave a pleased smile and winked at Marissa. "Lennie, no matter how much we know, there's always something new to learn. Something new is always going on, and people find out new ways to do things, and we teachers need to know about them."

"Oh … Well, if you won't be teaching, you can play with me more, isn't that right?"

"Yup, that's right. We can play more when I'm on sabbatical—that's what they call my time off."

"Sab-bat-ical? That's a funny word."

Not so funny, little guy. Charlie nodded and hugged Lennie again. *I worked my tail off for this.*

"Well, we can all play together longer each day," said Marissa. "Now Lennie, you're to get ready for school."

"I don't wanna go to school. Daddy doesn't have to go."

Oh, great, a fine way to start the new school year, Marissa and Charlie told each other in their glances.

"Lennie, you're going to be in the first grade now," Marissa reminded him, rubbing his back gently and leading him to his room. "Remember we've been talking about that. You'll do more grown up things, like reading books all by yourself. You're not in kindergarten any more. That was for little kids. You'll be seeing your friends, too."

"Oh, yeah, my friend Jimmy! I want to see Jimmy! I want to see if he has a backpack like mine." With that, Lennie rushed to find his school bag.

Whew. Both parents sighed and rolled their eyes.

Once Lennie was at school Charlie wandered around the house aimlessly, feeling lost without his normal schedule and commitments. "Gosh, Hon, it feels like the rug's been pulled out from under me."

"Just unwind and enjoy yourself during these first few weeks, dear. It'll come to you soon enough what you have to do. Think of that proposal you wrote out when you applied for this leave. It's going to be a big change at the beginning, so take it easy and mull over things."

"Yeah, just imagine, with nothing I *have* to do for a while … I think I'm going to like goofing off like this."

"Well then, let me fix you a good breakfast to start off your sabbatical, Dear. How about waffles and bacon and eggs?"

"Hey yeah, go ahead and spoil me."

One afternoon Charlie found himself sitting in his living room with three other musicians playing a Haydn string quartet. He was cheerfully musing to himself, *Ah, this is the life.…free to indulge in doing the thing I love most of all, playing string quartets. Plus, I have a little family, we live in a nice home in a modern city. What more can a man ask for? I love my teaching and the time for more research. I'll have to start going to the archives in Reno next month. Yup, it's been a long haul…these past seven years.*

Charlie's thoughts found their way back to the music, and he concentrated on his playing now with a couple of visiting musicians from California. They had just started the lively, upbeat allegro movement of the Haydn.

Hmm. Good composer, this Haydn. Yeah, real good; and solid, too. A lot of substance in his writing. Other composers of this period didn't develop each movement this thoroughly. Listen to this fugal passage…each instrument echoing the theme stated by the second violin, and taking turns. Wow, he manages to keep it so logical, yet sound so lyrical. He sure studied the Bach fugues thoroughly. Must be Bach's sons who spread the old man's art as they worked around Europe for various sponsors, Dukes, and Archbishops—the kinds of people we no longer have. What a harrowing situation that Bach's works were all but forgotten, then miraculously discovered by Mendelssohn when he noticed Bach's manuscripts used as wrapping paper by his family's butcher...bizarre.

"Un-nn," the first violinist murmured softly when Marissa was duetting perfectly as one voice with him on his melody approaching the end of the movement.

This snapped Charlie out of his reverie about the mastery of Franz Joseph Haydn's writing.

What the??? This violinist guy sounds like he's enjoying something sensual. Of course, I would, too the way we all sound, seamlessly harmonizing or replying to each other.

Marissa was playing second violin to a fine violinist from the Santa Barbara Symphony who suddenly appeared with a letter of introduction the day before, and they'd hurriedly set up this session.

Some time ago Charlie and Marissa registered their names with an agency for traveling musicians who wished to play chamber music when they came to Las Vegas. In the summer, when major symphonies around the country were on break, Marissa and Charlie received several calls from such visiting musicians. It was good to meet most of them, but they found a few to be somewhat dull, and had considered dropping their names from the listing. Today's group, fortunately, happened to be an especially good one. The cellist was in Las Vegas on a gambling spree, but played divinely. Charlie and Marissa had heard about his habit from friends in Chicago. Or was it Cleveland? No matter. He added so much to the group, and made them all feel as if they had been playing together for years and years. Every once in a while, this type of random meeting would occur, making all the players wish they had met much earlier.

When musicians play a string quartet, they start the brisk first movement, listening and feeling each other for their musicality, drawn to each other's deep love for music.

Formerly familiar passages become a revelation, as if there is something new arousing each player and drawing out a more energetic style of playing. This charges up each member of the group that has now become close to being electrified. These rare moments are what ensemble players live for. It is the ultimate soul-satisfying moment that a musician can experience, a magical moment that makes him grateful to be alive.

They go on to the second movement, usually a quiet, somber one. At the end of it, there is silence, all four sitting quietly as at the end of a prayer, not wishing to break the spell. All during the second movement, with each player in a hushed mood to match the music, Charlie tells himself that never has he been this happy in his life, that he must have died and gone to heaven.

Marissa watched her husband's blissful expression and sensed that this augured well for this coming year.

As the quartet was going into the third movement, a minuet, Marissa looked at Charlie, whose eyes shined brightly. She nodded her head and smiled invitingly as if to say "let's dance, my love."

Charlie beamed back, as if to say "yes, let's dance, just you and I."

As the music was coming to its end in the last allegro movement, all the players knew the elation of having performed consummately well. Each was totally immersed in the act of creating something with others of like mind. How ideal the world would be if people could work side by side in such harmony.

This is what Beethoven had in mind when he wrote his gigantic masterpiece, the Ninth Symphony. Bach expressed the same ideals in his St, Matthew Passion and the b minor Mass, works so grand and powerful that the performers and audience are transfixed after the sacred sounds have faded, still echoing in the listener's ear. With today's string quartet session, Marissa and Charlie felt as if they had entered the never-never land of Euphoria.

Chapter 27

Obon in Las Vegas, August 2000

Good afternoon, ladies and gentlemen. Welcome to our annual Obon Festival."

Applause rang from the three hundred people seated in folding chairs in a high school cafeteria converted for the Buddhist holiday celebration. The speaker was a prominent member of the Las Vegas Japanese-American community. He bowed to the now silent group, putting his speech on the podium. Clearing his throat, he began:

"As many of you know, Obon is one of the most important holidays in Japan, and the Issei have carried the tradition to this country. During Obon in Japan, workers are given a week's leave to return to their ancestral homes to observe this festival with their families. There, tradition holds that the spirits of their ancestors return to visit their families for three days. They are welcomed back by the living, who set places for them at the dining table with their favorite foods. Here today, we simply gather as a Japanese-American community to observe this holiday and to replicate some of the activities that are part of the celebration in Japan, mainly the Obon dancing.

"In recent years, *taiko* groups have sprung up in major cities in America, and I am proud to say that we have an excellent group here. *Taiko* accompaniment has always been part of the music at all Obon festivals, and our group will be performing for you in a few minutes."

The audience was seated in three or four rows on the outer edges of the huge room. Sitting in the third row, Marissa, Charlie, and Lennie turned toward a door from which drums of all sizes were being rolled over the hardwood floor to the center of the empty space in the middle of the cafeteria. First came the main drum, carefully pushed by two drummers. It was a huge barrel-shaped drum on its own wooden stand, standing a good seven feet high. Next came four smaller drums and a half dozen miniature ones. Lennie, at twenty years old, was beside himself with excitement. If the *taiko* group had not been performing, he knew that he would never be attending such a function with his parents. They were so old-fashioned, and liked these events with ice-age traditions that were so interesting to them. At least the *taiko* players were "with it." He liked their jazz-like compositions with bold, punctuated, modern beats.

Charlie tapped Lennie's shoulder excitedly. "Look son, there's Dan Morgan, the tympanist in our university orchestra. He's one of the drummers here!"

"Wow!" Lennie gasped. "That's neat. He's new at school, so I haven't talked to him yet. I've just seen him around campus. And look, Dad, there are girls—four of them in this group of ten. Don't they look awesome? I sure like their *happi* coats with their logo design."

For the next half hour Lennie sat spellbound listening to the primitive sounds booming from the various drums. Along with the rest of the audience, he seemed hypnotized by the deep, rumbling heartbeat rhythms, and was totally fascinated by the occasional dance steps of the leading drummer. Most of the time this drummer stood with his legs spread very wide, then would suddenly do marching steps as he twirled his sticks over his head and shouted. The other drummers followed suit, moving and shifting their weight at different times.

Marissa glanced at Charlie, who gave an understanding nod. They both knew that this would probably be one of the last times the three of them would enjoy a day together. After all, their son was now a young man, very much in his own world.

After the rousing beats of the finale, Lennie jumped up shouting "Bravo, Dan!" Surprised, Dan turned and waved, acknowledging Lennie's "thumbs up." The entire audience stood, smiling and clapping enthusiastically. "They were hip! Huh, Dad, Mom? I'm glad you brought me here!"

"Gee, Charlie, maybe we should have had Lennie take *taiko* lessons along with his piano lessons," said Marissa.

"Maybe," agreed Charlie. "Anyway, just be glad that he graduated as a computer engineer, and loves his work. At least he'll always have his good background as a pianist."

As the drums were rolled out of the room, the sound man prepared to put on CD's of Japanese Obon music, and was testing the volume. Charlie looked at Marissa and said, "Get ready to jump from that jarring blast, Hon. I don't think there ever was a rehearsal for our shows where the audio man didn't fool around and end up getting feedback."

Marissa laughed, but just then, came the screeching sound, and it startled everyone in the cafeteria. She shook her head and said, "Like old times, isn't it?"

"Oh, yeah," Charlie sighed. "All those years, making music on the Strip or at the college. I'm glad we're retired and Lennie's finished his schooling now, heading for Silicon Valley." He then reflected with a note of sadness, "Time sure flies. I have half a mind to move back to California."

"I wouldn't mind," said Marissa. "I always missed the cosmopolitan atmosphere that Vegas never had. The San Francisco area…."

"And now, let us begin the dancing," announced the emcee. "First, we shall present Mrs. Makino and her *odori* (dance) students in one of the traditional Obon dances, and after that you are all welcome to join in." About thirty dancers dressed in cotton summer kimonos and several others in more elaborate silk kimonos made their way to the floor and formed a large circle.

Lennie stood up and said meekly, "Hey, Mom, Dad, I'm going to talk to the *taiko* players and then see if Dan wants to hang out, okay?"

Charlie cleared his throat. "Okay, but come back because I'd really like the three of us to do one dance together. It will be for your Grandpa George and your Grandma Tomiko."

Lennie had started to pout, but the mention of his favorite grandfather, George Ohara, made him nod agreeably.

"Oh, yeah…Grandpa, *Ojiisan*…and Grandma, *Obaasan*. Boy, I sure miss them a lot. How long have they been gone now?"

"Almost three years for Grandpa and six years for Grandma," said Marissa. "Like Dad said, we'd like to do one dance together as a family, then you and your friend can go somewhere else."

There was still time before the audience would be joining in the dance, so Lennie went off to find the *taiko* group. Marissa and Charlie watched the student dancers who started performing with their teacher in precise uniform steps and moving in a counterclockwise direction. "Very good, aren't they? Think we can do that?" Charlie asked.

"Certainly not that well because we never came to any of the practice sessions, but if we copy the person in front of us, it'll be fun!."

Lennie returned with Dan as the students were finishing their performance. "Hello, Professor Lyons, Mrs. Lyons," said Dan, smiling but dropping his eyes.

"Hi, Dan, good to see you," said Charlie. "You were great in the ensemble work with the *taiko* group. We didn't realize you would be in it."

"Oh, uh, thank you, sir…. Uh, well, I'm an army brat. My Dad was in Japan for ten years before he was transferred here last year to Nellis Air Force Base. He and my mom encouraged my sister and me to learn all we could about Japan and the other countries where Dad was stationed. I loved the *taiko*, and even enrolled in a class, so I've been doing this for some time now."

"Now, ladies and gentlemen, please take your places around the circle."

Many from the audience, half of them men, hurried to the floor, making three smaller circles. Most wore *happi* coats, the loose-fitting lightweight cotton jacket tied in the front. They were in many different colors such as purple, blue, and red, and they had the names of the home temple printed in English on the back. It was surprising that these people had come from faraway states and even from Hawaii. Las Vegas itself had a population of about a thousand Japanese-Americans. There were a couple of young mothers with babes in arms, smiling and already doing some dance steps. The little girls liked dressing in their red kimonos and looked anxious to imitate the motions of their parents. Least enthusiastic were the little boys, suspicious about this kind of party, even if they had been given ice cream a little while ago. They were standing still with downturned mouths.

A high-pitched female voice came over the sound system singing with a *shamisen* accompaniment with occasional flute and *taiko* sounds in the background. (The shamisen is a 3-stringed, plucked banjo-shaped instrument.)

Dan jumped up and said to Lennie, "Come on. Let's all of us get into this circle. Len, you get behind me and imitate my motions as closely as you can." He then turned to Charlie and Marissa and said shyly, "Uh, Professor and Mrs. Lyons, I think you can see what I'm doing from where you are standing, so as I told Len, just try to make the same moves that I make." As the three people lined up behind him, he said, "This is an easy one. Also, everyone, smile as you dance. They believe in Japan that it's important to smile because it shows that you feel the joy of being with your departed ones who've come back to visit you."

Marissa, Charlie, and Lennie were all eager to dance but felt awkward as they raised their arms and made curving motions with their wrists as gracefully as they could. Strains of the *shamisen* music were dominant in this piece. As the singer chimed in, they imitated Dan's three steps forward, then backward—and bumped into each other, trying not to laugh at themselves. The steps were repeated, and by the end of the song Charlie gushed, "All those different body movements loosened me up. I'm really enjoying this! Thanks, Dan."

Dan blushed and smiled at the professor.

The next song started immediately, and everyone danced with much more assured movements: forward, backward, and arms waving gracefully.

Marissa remembered to smile and began thinking of her father. *Papa, thank you so much for all you've done for me.* Dancing like this had a way of consoling her more than the visits to his grave over the years. *And Papa, I brought my dear husband and your precious grandson to honor you today. They have done well, and I wanted you to see them as they are. Thank you, Papa, for all that you and Mama have sacrificed for me so that I can live meaningfully. I have had a good life with my husband. Your grandson is on the threshold of a promising life. He was able to finish college without interruption, and hopefully will have a good future. Thank you again, Papa ... And Mama, I feel so close to you today. For all the care you and Papa gave me as I was growing up, I can never thank you enough for doing it with so much love.* Tears filled Marissa's eyes.

Charlie, too, remembered to smile as he continued to dance. *This is something like a Memorial Day ritual, only with a Japanese accent ... Pop, thank you for all the guidance you have given Marissa and me all those years when we were building our lives here. I sure was scared of you at first, but grew to love and respect you ... Lennie adored you, misses you, and is surely grateful for all the wonderful times he had with you. Thank you, Pop, thank you.*

Lennie was starting to feel more familiar with the dance movements. "Smile," Dan reminded him. "I think you're getting the hang of this. Not too shabby."

"I'm actually starting to like this," Lennie replied "And I want to stay till the end. Hey, you even move like a native, and you don't really look Japanese with your blond hair," he quietly teased Dan. "I'm glad I'm standing right behind you like this. Cripes, ya know, I didn't want to come at all, but Dad started to twist my arm. Well, now I'm glad I tagged along. In fact, my folks'll faint when I tell them I'm going to stay and dance until the very end."

Dan moved back to dance alongside Lennie, saying, "I got a good dose of their culture, Len, and sometime soon I'll show you my album of our years in Japan." Then he added enviously, "You should look into your heritage some more. It's awesome—and different!"

When the music stopped, Charlie said to Marissa, "Hon, I want to keep dancing. I like the way dancing makes me feel, even if I look pitiful—there's something primal about moving and swaying around, and dancing with a crowd."

"Okay, you keep on then dear," Marissa replied with a smile. "I think I'll stop for now and just watch my two men dance."

Again, there was the musical introduction to another dance, with the sing-songy high-pitched female voice and the sounds of flute, *shamisen*, and faint drumbeats. Dan said to Lennie, "Here we go again, this is like the first number. Smile away, Len."

Lennie was indeed smiling as he waved his arms more

confidently and hummed along with the music. *"Granpa, Granma, they say you're both visiting us today. I believe it, and think it's really neat. When I was little, I always loved going to Monterey where you took me to the Dennis The Menace Park and Granma made the best sushi and cookies for me. And those Japanese fairy tales you both used to read to me too, some of it in Japanese so I'd get to hear the language that kids over there spoke. Oh, I miss those days. It hurts ... You always made me feel so special, and the way you would take turns hugging me. Thank you, Granma. Thank you, Granpa ... I'll try to become the gentleman you were. You are my hero, Granpa ... Granpa George. . .*

Acknowledgements

Dear Readers,

This book started as a legacy project for my children and grandchildren. At first, it was merely a binder filled with typewritten stories about my life, and of the more interesting people and places I'd known. As I kept adding anecdotes, I began to sense the need for them to know more about their heritage and about the Japanese immigrants who came to this country in the 20th century, eager to partake in the American Dream.

I began attending writer's groups in Las Vegas in the 1990's, at a time when electronic instruments started replacing live musicians on The Strip. Of greatest help to me initially was Alice Pasupathi, a thoughtful and perceptive writer who encouraged my beginning efforts. When she moved away, I met a talented instructor at a Border's Bookstore class, John H. Long (*The Heritage of Yawnogard*) along with new writer friends Ginger, Phil, Jerry, JoAnn, Nancy, and Troy, who gave me suggestions of immeasurable value.

Now, living in California, my biggest supporters are Cathy Jo Cress (*Mom Loves You Best*), Martha Alderson (*The Plot Whisperer*), Anne Beggs, Connie Leas (*Art of Thank You*), Patricia Ihrig, and Dolphin. Since I am not a writer, I depend heavily on critiques from these friends who are professionals in the writer's world.

A writer who went far beyond my request for help was Franz Steidl (*Lost Battalions*), when he generously took it upon himself to proofread and edit many chapters of my manuscript. I am forever grateful for his expertise and suggestions for this book.

Over the years, a variety books have appeared on the subject of Japanese immigrants living in America that poignantly describe the grimness of life and their struggles and sacrifices. While writing this book, their writings stirred buried memories, and spurred me on to writing about my own experiences. I hope that those of you interested in reading more about our small group of Americans will read these fine books: *Looking Like the Enemy*, by Mary Matsuda Gruenwald; *Nisei Linguists*, by James C. McNaughton about the MIS (Military Intelligence Service) men who served in the South Pacific; *Fighting for Honor*, by Michael L. Cooper; *A Time To Choose*, by Dr. Edward Blight; Jamie Ford's *Hotel on the Corner of Bitter and Sweet*; Karen Tei Yamashita's excellent *I Hotel*, and finally, the totally fearless novel ,*The Buddha in the Attic*, by Julie Otsuka, a hard hitting book that bowled me over. Otsuka's punches are haymakers. She tells the truth and spares no one.

Google®, YouTube® and Viewzi® provided me with countless facts with which I was able to weave this many-sided story.

For the production of a book, something I never dreamt of engaging in, my deepest thanks go to my editor, Cindie Farley, who proofed the manuscript assiduously for many long hours. To my expert publisher, Patricia Hamilton, whose experience and insights guided me to create a real book that I can hold in my hands and pass down to those dearest and closest to my heart, my small family. My sons deserve special mention, starting with Vince DiBiase, a holographer, who offered the ChromaGram print on the back cover. My thanks also to my younger son, David DiBiase, for his reactions and probing thoughts about Japanese–Americanism and all its effects on our lives. To his artist friend, Cheryl Puckett, the biggest 'thank-you' for her exceptional bookcover.

Recently, I joined the Watsonville–Santa Cruz JACL Senior Club. There, I met Mas and Marcia Hashimoto, community leaders who are involved with the Nisei in a wide range of activities, both culturally and politically, from local picnics to passage of legal measures in Washington, D.C. Also at the Senior Club, I met several men who had served in the highly decorated 442nd Infantry Regiment. Their story and that of the 100th Infantry Battalion from Hawaii is familiar to all older Japanese–Americans. Their heroism and sacrifice is a tremendous source of pride for all of us, and the ultimate vindication of Japanese–American loyalty and patriotism.

In my book, I write about the interpreters in the MIS who served in the Pacific War Theater under General Douglas MacArthur. For providing me with information about his training and work, I am indebted to the late George Iwao Yamamoto who patiently answered my questions week after week at the Senior Club. My brother, Satoru Yoshizato, began his service in the MIS at the end of WW II, and served in Korea and Japan after the war. Since both men's work was classified, I gleaned facts about the routines of the workplace and set their actions into parts of the wartime chapters.

Throughout my book, the facts about the evacuation camps and the musical workplace in Las Vegas are as accurately told as I can recall.

I would welcome any comments from you by e-mail: stories.eiko@yahoo.com

Eiko Ceremony, December 2012

Made in the USA
San Bernardino, CA
15 January 2014